Teaching the Bible to Children

Other books by the author
available from Marshall Pickering

ASSEMBLY PRAISE
QUOTATIONS FOR ALL OCCASIONS
THEMES FOR FAMILY WORSHIP

Teaching the Bible to Children

TONY CASTLE

Marshall Pickering
An Imprint of HarperCollins*Publishers*

Marshall Pickering is an Imprint of
HarperCollins*Religious*
Part of HarperCollins*Publishers*
77–85 Fulham Palace Road, London W6 8JB

First published in Great Britain
in 1993 by Marshall Pickering

13 5 7 9 10 8 6 4 2

Copyright © 1993 Tony Castle

Tony Castle asserts the moral right to be
identified as the author of this work

A catalogue record for this book is
available from the British Library

ISBN 0 551 02659-6

Printed and bound in Great Britain by
The Bath Press Limited, Bath, Avon

Dedicated to
Sharon and Earl Dierks

Contents

Acknowledgements

The author would like to thank the following for permission to use their copyright material.

North American Liturgy Resources for the words of the refrain, by Michael Joncas, from his song, "On Eagle's Wings".

Unless otherwise stated, biblical extracts are taken from the Good News Bible copyright Old Testament © American Bible Society, New York, 1976, Deuterocanonical Books/Apocrypha © American Bible Society, New York 1979. New Testament © American Bible Society, New York 1966, 1971, and 4th edition 1976. British usage edition of the Bible first published 1976. These extracts are used by kind permission of the American Bible Society and the British & Foreign Bible Society.

Introduction

GENERAL THOUGHTS:

This book brings together the two most important possessions of the Christian community; the word of God found in the Bible and the life of God found in our children, the hope of our future.

To have a Christian future our children must be familiar with the word of God, but to many of them the word, "Bible" spells boredom. In this age of over-stimulation by continual television in most homes, the very idea of studying the Bible is deadly dull and irrelevant to "real" life. If in their school life children of eight to twelve are learning through activity-based work and then arrive in a church setting where they are treated as mini-adults, there is further rejection. Children learn best when "doing" not when being talked at. Some of the latter is inevitable, but church leaders and teachers have often placed too much value upon the spoken word.

Active, committed Christians know that the Bible is not an object to be studied like some cherished, priceless fossil to be found in one of our museums; on the contrary, "the word of God is alive and active" (Hebrews 4:12), it exists to teach us now, to reveal God and his will for us now, to be "Sharper than any double-edge sword, which penetrates even to dividing soul and spirit" now.

If we have failed and are failing to reveal the dynamic nature of God's word, perhaps it is because we have tried to teach the Bible to children. We should instead be exposing our children to the Bible so that the word of God itself "speaks" to them and teaches them. We should not lose sight of the fact that the Bible is not an end in itself, but a vibrant means of coming to know, love and serve God, who alone is the Alpha and the Omega, "the first and the last, the beginning and the end" (Revelation 22:13).

PRACTICAL THOUGHTS:

In this book the effort has been made, through three terms of lessons, to try to "expose" children of eight to twelve to God's word, from the opening text to the closing memory verse. Through thirty-six lessons over 240 texts are used, in and through sixty-eight activities, which do not include Bible searches and learning sixty-three new words. From examining garden snails (in lesson 3, Made in God's Image) to racing ships to Tarshish (in lesson 22, on Jonah and his great fish) a wide range of activities has been proposed.

Old-fashioned learning by rote has been included too, with the children being introduced, each lesson, to words that adults might assume that they know. These can be copied out and learnt at home. The riches of the Psalms are made available each time in the form of a final prayer, which again can be copied out and used throughout the week as a personal prayer. Finally, closing hymn suggestions are offered from *Junior Praise* and *Mission Praise*.

It must be stressed that these thirty-six lessons are not a syllabus or even a programme; they are individual lessons which work better together but will work on their own. The author offers them as suggested outlines. The leader/teacher must think the lesson through and then adapt the material to the size of the class, the age range and the availability of materials, premises, etc. It is essential that the lessons are not taught straight from the book; they must become the teacher's own by, if necessary, adding or subtracting material. The person of the teacher, the children's greatest resource, should shine through, for the children will come to the word of God as surely through the faith of the teacher as through any number of structured Bible lessons.

Tony Castle
HARVEST 1992

Term One

GENESIS

LESSON 1:	# *In the Beginning*

AIM:	To help the children to understand that God is not like us, bound by time and change. He was there at the beginning, he is unchanging and will continue to exist when the world comes to an end.
AIDS:	A selection of old birthday cards. An alarm clock (old-style, with the two bells on top, or something similar is preferable).
PREPARATION:	None.
OPENING ACTIVITY:	*(Cards are passed round for the children to inspect.)* As you can see, these are birthday cards. Why do we send birthday cards? To celebrate a friend's birthday. We are happy that s/he was born, is alive and with us. Birthdays mark a beginning. We all have a birthday; for all of us there is a beginning day. We know that Jesus had a birthday (When do we celebrate that birthday?), but did God? Could you send a birthday card to God? No, because God had no beginning.
NEW WORDS:	Our Christian prayers and hymns use unusual words like, "Almighty", "Eternal" and "Infinite". What do these mean? Almighty – This comes from two words: "all" and "might"; it means that God can do everything, he is all-powerful. Eternal – This means without beginning or end: so God is eternal, without beginning or end. Infinite – The word "finite" means to have an end or a limit; so the word "infinite" means to have no limit or boundaries in time or space. So we can say, "God's power is infinite." Let's write those new words down, with their meanings, so that you can learn them at home.
PRESENTATION:	We saw how birthdays remind us of our beginning, the day we were born and the "world" began for us. What does this alarm clock remind you of? Yes, the beginning of a new day: we always associate an alarm clock with getting up in the morning and the start of a new day. If I wind up this clock *(match action with words)* and set the alarm to go off in five-minutes' time, I am winding it up NOW, but it will go off in the FUTURE. I have finished winding up the clock . . . there it is; the winding up is in the PAST. Time is made up of three parts: future, present (or NOW) and past; and it does not stay still. God is so wonderful, so almighty, that he is outside of time. We believe that he has no future, and no past; everything is NOW for God. When time began, "In the beginning . . ." God was already there; he is with us now and he will continue when this earth comes to an end. God is eternal; God has infinite power. Hard to understand? Yes, but we must do our best to understand while we place our trust in God and believe. *(Alarm goes off.)* The ringing of the bell was happening NOW. It has passed, and we can remember hearing it, but it has gone: it is in the PAST. God does not have to look back and remember . . . all is NOW.

12

TEXT:	*In the beginning God created the heavens and the earth.* Genesis 1:1

PRACTICAL ACTIVITY:

On the sheet of plain paper provided draw a large clock. It should have a large face and a base or support, like this. Draw no figures on the face.

Now that you have drawn the clock, put the following letters where numbers would be: B E G I N N I N G and E N D. On the base of the clock, outside of the face, write the word G O D.

Has anyone any idea what we are trying to "say" with our drawing? Yes, there was a time when God started to create – the beginning; and one day the time will come when the world will end. God is not on the clock because he is outside of time; he upholds creation and time.

BIBLE SEARCH:

We have spent time thinking about the words "In the beginning . . .", the first few words of the Bible.

Now look up and write down the last eleven words of the Bible: above them you will read "Come, Lord Jesus". God's wonderful creation will only be complete when Christ the Lord comes in glory at the end of the world.

Find Job 38:4. What question does God ask Job? Please write out the answer.

LOOKING FORWARD:

There is one other place in the Bible where you will find a book of the Bible starting with the words, "In the beginning . . ." It is the opening few words of John's gospel. John wants to tell us that when the Son of God became a human being, like us, a new creation story was about to unfold. Look up the gospel of John 1:1.

PSALM FOR THE WEEK:

Copy out these words and try to use them in your own prayers each day this week.

O LORD, you live for ever;
long ago you created the earth,
and with your own hands you made the heavens.
They will disappear, but you will remain;
they will all wear out like clothes.
You will discard them like clothes, and they will vanish.
But you are always the same, and your life never ends. Psalm 102:25–7

MEMORY VERSE:

With your own hands you made the heavens.

CLOSING HYMN:

If you close your lesson with a hymn, one of the following may be suitable. All from *Junior Praise* (MP = *Mission Praise*).

He's got the whole wide world in his hands   JP78/MP225
All things bright and beautiful   JP6/MP23
For the beauty of the earth   JP48/MP152
He made the stars to shine   JP76

LESSON 2:   *Let There Be Light*

AIM:	To help the children to appreciate the importance of light in their lives and the powerful symbol of light used throughout the Bible.
AIDS:	A powerful spotlight or torch. Four pictures as noted below.
PREPARATION:	Find and mount large pictures of the sun or a bright-sunshine day; plants; animals; a summer's day on the beach.
OPENING ACTIVITY:	*(Shining the spotlight or torch up into the ceiling or roof.)* You can see how powerful this torch is; even when it is daylight you can see where the beam reaches. If it were completely dark now that beam would be our only light. Just like God on the first day of creation, I could turn it off or on. Now a question for you all. Before putting up your hand to tell me the answer, think about it for a moment. Why did God make the light first? Why did he not make the land first, or the plants? Yes, because all plants and animals need light, otherwise they will not grow.
NEW WORDS:	Creation – This comes from the word "create". God's work of making the universe is called "the creation". The word "create" is more powerful than the word "make". When you and I make something we use materials like paper, cardboard, string and things; God makes from nothing. In other words, when God creates he does not use anything that is already there. Let us now write down the words "creation" and "create", and their meanings to learn at home. Creation – God's work of making the universe out of nothing.
PRESENTATION:	The next thing we are going to do is to take a deep breath, hold our noses with finger and thumb (like this) and close our eyes. Let's see how long you can go without taking a breath or opening your eyes. It didn't last long, did it? That's because we need to breathe and we do not like to be in the dark. Air and light are very important to us. If we had no air we would die and we would find it hard to exist long in total darkness.
PRACTICAL ACTIVITY:	I have here four pictures. We will call them A, B, C and D. A is of a beach scene on a summer's day. B is of animals *(specify if possible)*. C is a picture of the sun. D is of plants *(specify)*. These pictures are in the wrong order. Using the paper and pencil provided put the pictures in the order in which God created them. For example, if you think God created humans to play on the beach first put A first, and so on. Then write a few words why you have chosen that order. I will come round and help you with that. The correct order, which most of you had, was C, D, B and A. Did you know that the

TEXT:	*And God said, "Let there be light,"* *and there was light.* Genesis 1:3

sun is the most important part of God's creation? Without it nothing would exist on our planet, Earth. The sun is 93 million miles away from us and light from it takes eight minutes to get here. The wonderful thing is that God has placed our planet at exactly the right distance from the sun. Any closer and it would be too hot for life on Earth, and any further away and it would be too cold. How wonderful God is.

BIBLE SEARCH:	We have seen how important light from the sun is for our lives. The idea that in the same way God himself lights up our lives is found throughout the Bible. Now look up and write out the following:
	    Isaiah 2:5
	    2 Samuel 22:29
	    Isaiah 9:2
	    Revelation 22:5

LOOKING FORWARD:	Let us read the text you have written out from the prophet, Isaiah:
	    The people who walked in darkness
	    have seen a great light.
	
	Can anyone tell me at what time of the year you will hear those words read in church? Yes, at Christmas time. The prophets promised that a light would come to brighten up their gloomy lives. Jesus, the Son of God, was promised. So it was that Jesus called himself "the light of the world". Look up John 8:12 and John 1:5.

PSALM FOR THE WEEK:	Copy out these words and try to use them in your own prayers each day this week.
	
	The LORD is my light and my salvation;
	  I will fear no one.
	The LORD protects me from all danger;
	  I will never be afraid. Psalm 27:1

MEMORY VERSE:	Let us all remember for the coming week the opening verse of that psalm: *The Lord is my light and my salvation.*
CLOSING HYMN:	This little light of mine JP258 Who put the colours in the rainbow? JP288 Colours of day dawn into the mind JP28 Keep me shining, Lord JP147

LESSON 3: *Made in God's Image*

AIM: To deepen the children's appreciation of their own and every person's dignity.

AIDS: A selection of garden snails in jam jars. A number of pictures of people (preferably children) from different continents and cultures.

PREPARATION: Mount the pictures, sufficient in number for the children to have three or four per group of children. Put the same number of snails in jars, one jar for each group. Sort the children into small groups of three or four.

OPENING ACTIVITY: Before we divide into our groups let us do the thumb test. Everyone hold your right thumb up for us all to see. From where I am standing all those thumbs look the same; but are they?

Now examine your own thumb; look at it very closely. You will see a pattern of swirling lines. That's your thumb print and it is unique; that means it is different from any other thumb in the whole world. You are unique.

NEW WORDS: Dignity – In the way we are using the word it means having an understanding or sense of your own worth; that you are uniquely created by God and cannot be replaced.

Soul – The spiritual part of each one of us, which is not our body and is the "real" me.

Let's write those new words down, with their meanings, so that we can learn them at home.

PRESENTATION: Let us now sit in the groups that we have arranged. You should have a piece of paper, with a pencil to write with.

We looked at our thumbs and realized that, although it is hard to see clearly, they are all different. We are all different; we know we are different from others. But is it the same for all of God's creations?

PRACTICAL ACTIVITY: I want you to do two things –

1. Tip the snails out on your table and put them up the right way (please do not crush or hurt them). Look carefully at their shells and write down, and draw if you wish, what you see. When you have examined them you can swop your snails with another group.

I would like each group to tell us what they discovered. For example, were they all the same size? Were the markings on each exactly the same?

What we have discovered is that every snail is different; every snail has a unique shell. Just as we have unique fingerprints, snails have unique shells. It is the same throughout God's creation.

If we are all different from one another, how can we all be made in the image and likeness of God? If we are all the same as God that would make us all the same as one another. Does God have a right thumb? Does God have a head and a body? *(Discussion with the class: bring out that God is the mighty, all-powerful Spirit, which has no body.)*

Now we come to the second thing I want you to do –

TEXT:	*Then God said, "And now we will make human beings; they will be like us and resemble us . . ." Genesis 1:26*

2. Look at the pictures of people on your table. How are they different from one another? Write down what you see. Together try to answer this question: How are those people made in the image and likeness of God?

    We have now discovered that God has made mankind in all sorts of shapes and sizes and colours of skin. He loves all he has made. We are like to God, not in our bodies, which are different from one another, but in our souls or spirits. We share with God the power to know and to love.

BIBLE SEARCH: Let us use our bibles to find other places where Man is described as being made in the image of God. Let us together look at:

Genesis 5:1
Genesis 9:6
1 Corinthians 11:7

LOOKING FORWARD: Jesus Christ was the most perfect man and the great apostle Paul writes about him as "the visible likeness of the invisible God. He is the first-born Son, superior to all created things" *(Colossians 1:15).*

PSALM FOR THE WEEK: Copy this psalm out to use as your prayer this week.

*O LORD, our Lord,
  your greatness is seen in all the world!
When I look at the sky, which you have made,
  at the moon and the stars, which you set in their places –
what is man, that you think of him;
  mere man, that you care for him?*

*Yet you made him inferior only to yourself;
  you crowned him with glory and honour.* Psalm 8:1, 3–5

MEMORY VERSE: Let us all try to remember through the week the words of praise:

*O Lord, our Lord,
  how majestic is your name in all the earth.*

CLOSING HYMN:

He gave me eyes so I could see   JP74
Two little eyes to look to God   JP262
If I were a butterfly   JP94

LESSON 4: *Man, Steward of Creation*

AIM:
To help the children appreciate the responsibility laid upon mankind for the care of God's creation.

AIDS:
A large card, with the diagram (right) clearly drawn on it. A large stone, a cabbage or similar vegetable; and an insect in a jar, or a snail. A willing pupil's pet, preferably a cat or dog.

PREPARATION:
Place the stone, cabbage and livestock in the care of individual pupils, who keep them with them in their usual place.

OPENING ACTIVITY:
Hands up those who have been given some thing or creature to look after. What have I done? Yes, I have trusted you with the care of those things. I decided that you were responsible enough to look after them for me. Hands up: Who can tell me what I would say or do if I found that one of you had failed my trust. Yes, would I be right to be angry?

   That is exactly what this lesson is about, because God has trusted mankind to look after all the animals and creatures in his world . . . and often people have failed his trust.

NEW WORDS:
Steward   – Someone who is trusted to look after another person's property.

Stewardship – Doing the work of the steward.

Let's write those new words down and learn them at home.

PRESENTATION:
We have read in Genesis how God, the Creator, made everything in a definite order, spreading his work over six days. His work started simply with the land appearing, then plants, then birds and fish, animals and finally as the pinnacle of his creation, mankind. Rather like this (*show and explain the diagram*).

PRACTICAL ACTIVITY:
Would the girl/boy with the stone please bring it up, show it to us all and place it on the table. That is the first rung on the ladder of creation. Notice that a stone is cold and still and lifeless.

   Now the pupil with the vegetable. This is different from the stone; it has a simple form of life inside it for it grows; but it cannot move around on its own.

   The insect, or snail, is different. It not only has life inside it, it can also move around on its own. But it is not so high a life-form as the pet which is now brought up for us to admire. A cat or dog is capable of some affection, which you would not expect from an insect.

   (*Looking at the diagram again*) Man is at the top; part of the animal kingdom but having "likeness to God" which we call a spirit or soul. We are at the top because we are trusted with the stewardship of God's creation.

   So that you do not forget our diagram I would like you to copy it on one side of the sheet of plain paper; the other side you will need for today's Bible work.

TEXT:

"Human beings will have power over the fish, the birds, and all animals, domestic and wild, large and small."
                                                                    Genesis 1:26

BIBLE SEARCH:

I want you now to find Psalm 8:6–9 and, on the plain sheet of paper I will provide, I want you to copy out those verses in the centre of the sheet. I would like you to decorate the margin or edge as beautifully as you can.

LOOKING FORWARD:

None.

PSALM FOR THE WEEK:

Copy out this psalm to use as a prayer this week.

To you alone, O LORD, to you alone
and not to us, must glory be given
because of your constant love and faithfulness.
Heaven belongs to the LORD alone,
   but he gave the earth to man.
Praise the LORD!   Psalm 115:1, 16, 18

MEMORY VERSE:

Let us try to remember these words:

To you alone, O Lord, to you alone
and not to us, must glory be given.

CLOSING HYMN:

All things bright and beautiful   JP6/MP23
Have you seen the pussy cat?   JP72
Who put the colours in the rainbow?   JP288

The Seventh Day

AIM: To help the children to come to a deeper appreciation of the special and important role of Sunday in the life of the Christian.

AIDS: Two placards, wording below.

PREPARATION: Divide the children into two groups (unless a very large number are involved). They go into these groups when it is time for the Practical activity. Keep them apart and prepare with each separately.

The first group: These represent the Jewish community. On their placard they write in bold letters the following:

Sabbath – The Jewish Holy Day on Saturday.
Each week we recall the work of creation.

The second group: These represent the Christian community. On their placard they write, boldly for all to see:

Sunday – The Christian Holy Day on the first day of the week.
Each week we recall the resurrection of Christ; the work of the new creation.

OPENING ACTIVITY: Can you all remember the Ten Commandments? One of them we Christians do not keep exactly as it is written. Do you know which one? Well, you have given some good ideas but the answer is the third Commandment, *Remember to keep holy the Sabbath day*. The Sabbath is Saturday and we, as Christians, keep *Sunday* holy.

NEW WORDS: Sabbath – The Jewish holy day which begins on Friday evening and finishes Saturday evening.

Observance – Means to notice and keep special. Sometimes used with the word "Sabbath" by people who want to keep a day special for God each week.

Let us copy out these new words to learn at home.

PRESENTATION: How many of you are up in the morning when your father goes out to work? It depends of course on his job, but your dad will dress for his work. For example, if he works for a telephone company he will wear the uniform they provide; if he works in an office he will wear a suit; and if he is a fireman he will put on that uniform. He goes off to work and hopefully returns satisfied with his day's work in the afternoon or evening.

When we read the first chapter of Genesis there is a lovely picture of God going to work each day; being pleased with his work at the end of the day.

Then God commanded, "Let the earth produce all kinds of plants, those that bear grain and those that bear fruit" – and it was done. So the earth produced all kinds of plants, and God was pleased with what he saw. Evening passed and morning came – that was the third day. Genesis 1:11–13

But on the seventh day he rested; he had the day off from work. From the beginning of their religion the Jews have always kept that day as a special day, when there was to be no work at all.

Jesus rose from the dead on the third day after his death, that is on the day after the Sabbath; the first day of the new week; the day we now call Sunday. The first Christians

TEXT:

God blessed the seventh day and set it apart as a special day,
because by that day he had completed his creation
and stopped working.   Genesis 2:3

used to keep holy the Jewish Sabbath AND the next day to celebrate the resurrection of Jesus. They stopped keeping holy the Sabbath when they stopped keeping the other Jewish laws.

PRACTICAL
ACTIVITY:

(The children go to their pre-arranged groups and start work on producing their placards. The groups should be kept apart so that neither sees the work of the other. An elder child should be taken out and given the following question to ask, "How do you make your day special for God?")

(The teacher will need to go to each group in turn and tell them to prepare, as a group, an answer to the question that will be asked of them. For example, the "Jewish" group will answer: By having a special Sabbath meal, when the food and the family are blessed; by walking to the synagogue on Saturday morning, and having a quiet family day with no work.)

(When the groups are ready the "Jewish" group should go first. While the others sit they stand in the front holding up their placard and are asked, "How do you make your day special?" and "Why is your special day on Saturday?")

(The groups change places and repeat the questions.)

BIBLE SEARCH:

Today I want you to look up Exodus 20:8–11 and write out what you find there. Also, look up Jeremiah 17:19–27 and answer this question, "What is threatened if the people do not observe the Sabbath?"

LOOKING
FORWARD:

Jesus spoke about the very strict way the Jewish leaders of his time kept the Sabbath. They did not want Jesus to even cure a person on that day. Read out Matthew 12:1–14. Jesus insists that love and concern for people comes before keeping rules about the Sabbath.

PSALM FOR
THE WEEK:

Copy out the following psalm to use as a prayer this week.

I wait patiently for God to save me;
   I depend on him alone.
He alone protects and saves me;
   he is my defender,
   and I shall never be defeated.

I depend on God alone;
I put my hope in him. Psalm 62:1, 2, 5

MEMORY
VERSE:

My soul finds rest in God alone.
I wait patiently for God to save me;
I depend on him alone.

CLOSING
HYMN:

> Morning has broken   JP166/MP467
> New every morning is the love   JP171/MP480
> This little light of mine   JP258

Woman: Man's Companion

AIM:	To show the children that it was God's plan from the beginning that woman should have equal dignity with man.
AIDS:	Paper and pencils for the children. Pictures of men: sports heroes, pop singers, etc. Pictures of women: fashion models, pop singers, etc.
PREPARATION:	Divide the children into two groups, boys and girls. Appoint a leader for each group.
OPENING ACTIVITY:	*(Give out the pictures of men to the boys' group and the pictures of women to the girls.)* I want you to pass round the pictures and talk about them among yourselves. I am going to ask you in a few minutes, what sort of person should the ideal man or woman be? *(Ask the question and receive comments and discussion. Start with the boys' group.)*
NEW WORD:	There is only one word to write out and learn this time.
	Equality – Accepting everyone as equal, treating them fairly and in the same way.
PRESENTATION:	Loneliness is something that everyone, old and young, experiences. Hands up if you have ever been lonely. I have and I know some housebound elderly folk who are very lonely.
	Because Adam, the first man, was lonely God created the animals to keep him company; but Adam did not find that they were suitable companions. So God created woman to be the companion of man.
PRACTICAL ACTIVITY:	On the paper provided write down what your ideal boyfriend would be like, if you are a girl; and your ideal girlfriend, if you are a boy. Please be sensible about this and don't write down silly answers which we cannot read out.
	Now put all the boys' answers together and all the girls' answers together. *(Ask the leader of each group to read out some of the comments collected together.)*
	At the time when the book of the Bible we call Genesis was written, women were being treated very badly as slaves. The writer, who expressed the word of God, showed that God had always intended woman to be a friend and companion to man, not a slave to be treated only a little better than an animal. Women have equal dignity with men.
	Just now both groups, boys and girls, were treated with equality; both groups gave their ideas and both were listened to in the same way. Boys are not better than girls and girls are not better than boys; both need one another. You showed this in the work you did on boyfriends/girlfriends.
	There is an old Jewish saying told by the rabbis that God did not take the bone from the man's foot to show that woman was to be trod on like a slave; or from the man's head to show that she was intended to "boss" men about. No, the bone was taken from close to the man's heart. This was to show that woman was to be the love-companion of man, always close to his heart as his equal.
BIBLE SEARCH:	Let us try to find some of the famous women of the Bible. Using the index to the Bible, look up a text that tells us a little about the person (for you to read out to the rest of us): Ruth; Esther; Mary, Mother of Jesus; Mary Magdalene.

TEXT:

"At last, here is one of my own kind –
Bone taken from my bone, and flesh from my flesh.
'Woman' is her name because she was taken out of man."

Genesis 2:23

LOOKING
FORWARD:

The men friends of Jesus all ran away when he was arrested and only the women stayed loyal to him; it was the women who were to be found at the foot of the cross when Jesus died. Their reward was that it was the women, Mary Magdalene and two others, who were the first to find the tomb of Jesus empty and Jesus risen from the dead.

PSALM FOR
THE WEEK:

Here is a psalm for you to copy out and use during the coming week.

Come, let us praise the LORD!
Let us sing for joy to God, who protects us!
Let us come before him with thanksgiving
and sing joyful songs of praise. Psalm 95:1–2

MEMORY
VERSE:

Come, let us praise the LORD!

CLOSING
HYMN:

He's got the whole wide world   JP78
For the beauty of the earth   JP48/MP152
I will sing, I will sing   JP126/MP99

LESSON 7: *Temptation*

AIM:	To develop the children's understanding of the nature and danger of temptation.
AIDS:	A container(s), box or basket, of attractively wrapped chocolates.
PREPARATION:	Depending on the number of children involved, arrange them into one or more circles, approximately eight per circle. Start the session with the chairs already set out.
OPENING ACTIVITY:	Today's lesson is about temptation. Now there is a big difference between being tempted to do something that is wrong and actually doing it. Everyone on this earth is tempted . . . but not everyone gives way to temptation. This morning's reading was about the first temptation which led to the first sin. But temptation does not have to lead to sin.
	I am going to pass round a box of chocolates that belong to me. You may not touch them, only look and pass them on. *(Suit action to words.)* Now we will pass them round again; this time you can put your hand in the box and touch the chocolates, but you must NOT take one.
	Let's talk about what we have done. Did anyone feel tempted to take one? Why did you not take one? Was it because I was watching? Can anyone describe the "feeling" of temptation? If you resist temptation how do you then feel?
NEW WORDS:	It's time to write down some new words to learn.
	Conscience – The "voice" or sense inside each person that tells what is right or wrong about thoughts and actions.
	Sin – A wrongdoing, breaking God's Commandments; "missing the mark" of the standards set for us by Jesus.
	Temptation – Being attracted or drawn to do something wrong.
PRESENTATION:	What was the fruit that the woman took from the tree? No, it does not say in the Bible that it was an apple. It just says "fruit" and it could have been any fruit, an orange or banana; we do not know. The thing is, it was attractive to the woman, who felt that she just had to have it. She did not resist the temptation but involved the man in her sin.
	Let us talk about what tempts people these days. Can you give me examples of wrong things that boys and girls of your age are tempted to do? How can we fight temptation? What should we do when we feel tempted? Would you pray for help?
PRACTICAL ACTIVITY:	As below.
BIBLE SEARCH:	Today we will combine our Practical activity and the Bible search. Find the following texts and then answer the question, "Who is being tempted?" In the gospel temptation, how could the temptation have been avoided?
	Job 1:6–22
	Zechariah 3:1–10
	Luke 22:3–6

TEXT:	*The snake asked the woman, "Did God really tell you not to eat fruit from any tree in the garden?"*
	Genesis 3:1

LOOKING FORWARD:	Before Jesus started his work as a preacher and teacher he was severely tempted. We are going to look at what happened to him. *(Read Matthew 4:1–11.)*

From that we can see how Jesus himself was tempted. We can pray to him when we are tempted because he knows what it is like. |
| PSALM FOR THE WEEK: | Copy this out and try to use it for your own prayer this week.

I call to you, LORD, help me now!
  Listen to me when I call you.

Lord, place a guard at my mouth,
  a sentry at the door of my lips.
Keep me from wanting to do wrong
  and from joining evil men in their wickedness.

I call to you, Lord; help me now!
  Listen to me when I call to you. Psalm 141:1, 3–4 |
| MEMORY VERSE: | *O Lord, listen to me when I call to you.* |
| CLOSING HYMN: | Will your anchor hold in the storms of life?   JP290/MP275
Your ways are higher than mine   JP295
We shall overcome   JP270
Love, joy, peace and patience, kindness   JP158
Father, lead me day by day   JP43 |

LESSON 8:   *The Fall*

AIM: To help the children to understand the origin of all sin in the world, Man's first disobedience.

AIDS: Large pictures, mounted on card, of road-traffic signs that give orders, e.g. STOP. Pictures, if possible, of the Leaning Tower of Pisa and the Eiffel Tower. (These can be drawn large from smaller photos.)

PREPARATION: None.

OPENING ACTIVITY: *(Show the road sign or signs.)* Where do you see these? What do they tell the driver to do? What will happen if the driver does not do as he is told? Yes, the police could arrest him because he could do something very dangerous.

What do we call it when we do something we are told not to do? No, the word I am thinking of is "disobedient", which is the opposite of "obedient". The driver who disobeys the traffic sign could cause an accident and be in serious trouble.

NEW WORDS: Write down the following words and learn them at home. We will have a test soon.

Obedient   – Doing what someone in authority, like a parent, teacher or policeman, tells us to.

Original Sin   – The name given to the first sin committed by mankind. Adam and Eve were disobedient.

Transgression – Another word for "sin".

PRESENTATION: This first picture *(showing it)* is of a famous tower in Paris. Does anyone know what it is called? The second tower is in Italy. Does anyone know what this one is called?

The first looks and is safe; the second looks and is dangerous. God made humans to love and obey him; to be upright, like the Eiffel Tower.

Sadly, you will remember, according to the story we have read in Genesis, the first humans disobeyed God. They did what they were told not to do. They leant towards evil, like this tower of Pisa.

PRACTICAL ACTIVITY: *(Arrange the children into two groups.)*
Group one, your leader will read out chapter 3 of Genesis again; then you must decide together what life was like in Paradise, before the sin of Adam and Eve. After ten minutes your leader will tell us what you have written down.

Group two, your leader will read out chapter 3 and you'll decide together how God punished Adam and Eve for their disobedience. You can tell us all in ten minutes' time what you have discovered.

We have heard from both groups. You can see that changes happened to God's world and the life of humans as a result of that first sin.

We have also been like the Leaning Tower of Pisa, since what is called the Fall, that is, the disobedience of Adam and Eve. We all find it easier to be bad than to be good; we have to struggle all the time to be good; we have this constant inclination or leaning towards evil.

TEXT:	*The woman gave some of the fruit to her husband,* *and he also ate it.* Genesis 3:6

BIBLE SEARCH:	This time we are going to combine our Bible search with Looking Forward.
	
	    The great teacher, the apostle Paul, told his friends that Jesus was like a second Adam; Jesus came and did exactly what God asked. Where the first Adam had been disobedient, Jesus, the second Adam, was obedient.
	
	    Look up the following and write out what you find:
	    Luke 2:51
	    Matthew 26:36–42
	    Matthew 28:20
	    Romans 5:2–21

LOOKING FORWARD:	As above.

PSALM FOR THE WEEK:	*Happy are those whose lives are faultless,*
	who live according to the law of the LORD.
	You are all I want, O LORD;
	  I promise to obey your laws.
	I ask you with all my heart
	  to have mercy on me, as you have promised Psalm 119:1, 57–58

MEMORY VERSE:	*You are all I want, O Lord.*
CLOSING HYMN:	Father, lead me day by day JP43 When the road is rough and steep JP279 Abba, Father, let me be JP2/MP1 Will your anchor hold in the storms of life? JP290/MP275

LESSON 9:   *My Brother's Keeper*

AIM:	To help the children to appreciate that Jesus called us to the essential virtue of brotherly love, the total opposite to that shown in mankind's first sin after the Fall.
AIDS:	A reader. A recording, if possible, of the song "He ain't heavy, he's my brother" by the Hollies (EMI EM74).
PREPARATION:	None.
OPENING ACTIVITY:	*(Read the story, Genesis 4:1–16. Ask questions to see that the children have understood.)* What work did Abel have? What did Cain do? Why do you think God accepted Abel's sacrifice but not Cain's? There is a lesson for us, in that God will not accept what is second best; God wants the best from us.
NEW WORDS:	Sacrifice – The giving or offering up of something of value, to get something of greater value. So, the offering of a gift to God to give him praise or ask for forgiveness.
	Propitiate – To try to put things right, or make up with God. Sacrifice was often made for this.
PRESENTATION:	*(Divide the children into two groups. Play the recording, or tell its story.)* We heard two stories: the first about a brother killing his brother out of jealousy; and the second, inspired by the teaching of Jesus, about a brother helping his brother. The second story reminds us of the story Jesus told about the Good Samaritan.
PRACTICAL ACTIVITY:	Each group will now put a little play together, for the rest of us to watch. The first group must base their play on the Cain and Abel story. The second group can chose either the story of the Good Samaritan or the story of the recording.
	You can clearly see how the teaching of Jesus is the complete opposite to the behaviour of those who lived after the Fall. Jesus calls each of us to imitate the love of the Good Samaritan.
BIBLE SEARCH:	The first letter of John is only five chapters long but there are about ten references in it to brotherly love. Find the letter and find as many of the references as you can. Start by reading 1 John 3:12. Choose and write out one that you think best shows us the teaching of Jesus.
LOOKING FORWARD:	None.
PSALM FOR THE WEEK:	*Praise the LORD!* *Give thanks to the LORD, because he is good; his love is eternal. Who can tell all the great things he has done? Who can praise him enough?* Psalm 106:1–2
MEMORY VERSE:	*Give thanks to the Lord, because he is good.*

TEXT:

The LORD asked Cain, "Where is your brother Abel?"
He answered, "I don't know. Am I supposed to take care of my brother?"

Genesis 4:9

CLOSING
HYMN:

When I need a neighbour   JP275
Bind us together, Lord   JP17
Make me a channel of your peace   JP161/MP456
Brothers and sisters   JP21

The Flood

AIM: To show that just as God, when faced with mankind's wrongdoing, made a new start, so can we.

AIDS: A bowl or bucket of water; a glass or cup. A large-format calendar, preferably with all the months to view.

PREPARATION: None.

OPENING ACTIVITY: *(Using a filled glass or cup, pour water, so that everyone can see it, into the remaining water in the bowl. A child could be invited to come out and do this.)* What do we use water for? *(Accept all answers – to wash, to drink, etc.)*

Can water ever be dangerous? *(Discuss the need to be able to swim.)* What happens if the water tank in your roofspace (loft) bursts open? What damage is caused when it floods the house?

So water can be used to save life – the need that plants, animals and we humans have to drink; and it can destroy.

NEW WORDS: Write down these words, which you may hear used in church, and learn them for next week.

Re-generate or Re-generation – To undergo a change of life; a new start or renewal.

Revival   – To bring life back again, renew or reawaken people's lives and their faith.

PRESENTATION: *(Ask the children to indicate when in the year there is, or could be, a new beginning. For example, 1st January, the beginning of the new school year, after the Easter holiday, etc.)* There are times when we have to stop, look at ourselves and make a new start. And that is what God, the Creator, did with the flood story: he made a new start.

Let us now read the story together: Genesis 6 and 7. *(Leave chapters 8 and 9 for lesson 11.)*

The story tells how God was so unhappy with the wrongdoing of humans that he decided to destroy what he had made . . . and start afresh. One man and his family were saved because they were good-living people.

Now I want you all to think before answering this question. When and how in *your* life does water finish off something then, afterwards, mark a new beginning? I'll repeat that . . . It's not so hard: when you come to the end of the day what happens? Yes, you have a bath or a wash before going to bed. When you get up in the morning what do you have to do? Yes, have another wash. So water gets rids of your dirtiness before going to bed and freshens you up ready for a new day. God decided to get rid of the world's dirtiness with the waters of the flood.

How do people become Christians? How do they wash away sin and make a new start as a child of God? Yes, through the waters of Baptism. Can you see how in the story of the flood God used water to wipe away sin? And how, when Jesus came, he gave us Baptism to be the sign of wiping out sin and making a fresh start?

TEXT:	*"I am going to send a flood on the earth to destroy every living being."*
	Genesis 6:17

PRACTICAL
ACTIVITY:
On the plain paper I would like two pictures: one at the top of the page showing the flood; one at the bottom showing a modern Baptism.

Then on the back of the piece of paper, at the top (behind the flood picture), I want you to write down one thing you are sorry for and would like to "wipe out" of your life. For example, being unkind to a brother or sister. At the bottom, behind the Baptism picture, one good resolution to "freshen up" your life.

BIBLE SEARCH:
Look up the following:
Ezekiel 36:25
John 3:5
Hebrews 10:22

LOOKING
FORWARD:
You will see from the two texts, John and Hebrews, how God planned to use water to be the sign of people's turning from sin.

PSALM FOR
THE WEEK:
As a deer longs for a stream of cool water,
so I long for you, O God.
I thirst for you, the living God;
when can I go and worship in your presence? Psalm 42:1, 2

MEMORY
VERSE:
I thirst for you, the living God.

CLOSING
HYMN:

If I were a butterfly   JP94
We really want to thank you, Lord   JP268/MP256
The greatest thing in all my life   JP239/MP219
Great is your faithfulness   JP64/MP62

LESSON 11: # God's Covenant with Noah

AIM: To explore with the children the concept of "covenant" and the first of an important series between God and his people.

AIDS: *(Arrange in advance.)* Pets of the children that can be easily brought to class, e.g. a hamster in its cage, without any undue conflict (e.g. avoid cats and dogs together). A big rainbow painted on to a large white card.

PREPARATION: Ask selected children, who have brought pets, to talk about them to the rest of the class.

OPENING ACTIVITY: *(The children, who have been prepared, tell the others about their pets.)* You have heard about some of the pets people have. You know there are lots of other pets people can have, for example, even snakes or spiders can be kept as pets. There is a special bond between a pet and its owner/keeper. God says that there should be a special bond between humans and animals. Let's read the story of the ark and its cargo of animals in the Bible: Genesis 7–9:17.

NEW WORDS: We have been learning new words for the last ten lessons. Next time, during lesson 12, we will have a test to see how many of those new words you can remember.

Write this new and important word down and learn it for next week.

Covenant – An agreement or contract between two people or groups. Another word which means the same is "Testament". So the first part of the Bible is about the old agreement or contract between God and his people, and the second part of the Bible (about Jesus and his teaching) is the new agreement between God and his people.

PRESENTATION: *(Displaying the rainbow.)* Can anyone tell me what God said, in the Bible, this would be a sign of? Yes, a sign of the agreement that God has made with the whole human race, and the animal kingdom, never again to destroy everything in a great flood.

Altogether there are seven covenants made by God in the first part of the Bible; some are more important than others. This is the first one.

Does anyone know how a rainbow happens? Yes, when there has been some rain and the sun shines brightly, it happens naturally. The coloured bands of the rainbow are caused by the bending of light rays from the sun as they enter the raindrops. A wonderful sign for God to use, which seems to link heaven and earth.

Let us use our Bible search time now to find other agreements or covenants between heaven and earth, God and his people.

PRACTICAL ACTIVITY: None.

BIBLE SEARCH: After Noah, the next most important person in the Bible is Abraham, and God made a covenant with Abraham. Look up Genesis 17. Write out the words of the agreement: what God promises and what Abraham is expected to do.

After Abraham, Isaac and Jacob, the next important leader of God's people was Moses, and God made a covenant with Moses. Look up Exodus 19, 20 and 24 *(teacher guidance*

TEXT:
"I am putting my bow in the clouds.
It will be the sign of my covenant with the world."

Genesis 9:13

required). Write out the words of the agreement: what God promises and what the Israelites are expected to do *(teacher guidance required).*

LOOKING FORWARD:
Now we come to the new agreement which is in the second part of the Bible. Look up Matthew 26:17–30. Write out verse 28.

Look up Luke 22:14–23. Write out verse 20.

You can see how Jesus makes a new covenant or agreement: "love one another" he says, "and I will be with you."

PSALM FOR THE WEEK:
Give thanks to the LORD,
proclaim his greatness;
tell the nations what he has done.
He will keep his covenant for ever,
his promises for a thousand generations.
He will keep the agreement he made with Abraham. Psalm 105:1, 8–9

MEMORY VERSE:
Give thanks to the Lord.

CLOSING HYMN:

Rise and shine, and give God his glory   JP210
Who put the colours in the rainbow?   JP288
Mister Noah built an ark   JP167
Oh, the Lord looked down from his window in the sky   JP184

The Tower of Babel

AIM:	To show that God punishes the proud and gives his Spirit to the humble.
AIDS:	Building bricks, as used by tiny children. Two volunteers to come out in public. Drawing paper and a picture of a Ziggurat (see any handbook of the Bible).
PREPARATION:	None.
OPENING ACTIVITY:	When you were very young many of you enjoyed building with wooden bricks, and then knocking them over again. We are now going to watch two volunteers see how high they can get with these bricks. *(This should be a fun event, so the children can be encouraged to call out support for the "builders". When the "tower" is as high as it will go it can be demolished.)*
	You saw how proud our volunteers were in succeeding to build the tower so high. That is fine here, but when men tried to reach up to heaven, God was not pleased that they were trying to be like gods. Let's hear the first part of the story: Genesis 11:1–4.
NEW WORDS:	None.
PRESENTATION:	Can anyone tell me about their language? What were the words they used, about the tower, which upset God? Yes, "So that we may make a name for ourselves."

Who can remember the lesson on Adam and Eve? What wrong thing were they tempted to do? What prompted them to commit that sin? Yes, disobedience. Now what is disobedience caused by? Pride, is the answer. That is the same human sin we have heard in the story of the tower: human pride.

PRACTICAL ACTIVITY: This is a picture of a Ziggurat *(show picture)*. A number of these tall towers have been found by archaeologists in Mesopotamia (modern Iraq). This is the sort of tower that the people in the story were trying to build. Under the heading "Tower of Babel" I'd like you now to copy it.

Let's hear the second part of the story: Genesis 11:5–9. What punishment did God impose? Their spirit of pride brought them disunity; and a babble (Babel) of different languages, so that they could not understand one another.

BIBLE SEARCH:	Look up and read Acts 2:1–12. Copy out verse 4.
LOOKING FORWARD:	What you have discovered is that when the friends of Jesus *humbly* did what God wanted – that is, go out and tell everyone about Jesus – the Spirit gave them the gift to be understood by everyone listening; no matter where they came from. That day, Pentecost day, showed how believing in the risen Jesus unites everyone and empowers people.
EVALUATION:	Last time I promised that we would have a little test to see if you could remember the important words we have learnt.
	On your own, on the paper provided, write down for me the meaning of the following words:

"Now, let's build a city with a
tower that reaches the sky . . ."
Genesis 11:4

Creation   Soul
Steward   Conscience
Temptation   Sacrifice
Covenant

PSALM FOR
THE WEEK:

Sing a new song to the LORD;
    he has done wonderful things!
By his own power and holy strength
    he has won the victory.
The LORD announced his victory;
    he made his saving power known to the nations.
Psalm 98:1–2

MEMORY
VERSE:

Sing a new song to the Lord.

CLOSING
HYMN:

All over the world the Spirit is moving   JP5/MP18
Spirit of the living God fall afresh on me   JP222/MP613
Bind us together, Lord   JP17/MP21

Term Two

ANIMALS IN THE BIBLE

LESSON 13: *The Naming of the Animals*

AIM: To show the children how God involved mankind in his work of creation; and how humans and animals are bound together in a relationship of care and trust.

AIDS: Pets, as below. Picture of a Dodo.

PREPARATION: In advance, invite the children to bring their pets for this lesson (as long as they can sensibly be brought along, e.g. a pony might be a bit difficult). Selected young people will be asked to talk to the others about their pets.

OPENING ACTIVITY: *(The chosen pupils, in turn, speak about their pets: how long they have had them; what they feed them; and finally and importantly, how the pet's name was chosen, and why.)* Let's now find out the names of all the other pets here today.

One of the first things that we all do when we get a pet is to choose a name for it, then the bond between us and our pet begins to grow.

NEW WORDS: Steward and Stewardship – The word "steward" is like the word, "manager". A manager does not own the place where he or she works; he has the task of "looking after". So a steward is someone who looks after something for someone else; in this case, for God.

Copy out the meaning of "steward/stewardship" to be learnt at home.

PRESENTATION: Did your parents get you the pet and then ask you to give it a name? Or did they get it, name it themselves and then give it to you? Isn't it usually the first way, *you* choose the name? That is what God did. He did not need the man's help but he wanted Adam to feel that he was really important and could work with God . . . when invited to. So Adam named the animals.

Looking back over thousands of years, do you think mankind has done a good job looking after God's creation, especially the animals? *(Accept all kinds of ideas and comments.)*

 Does anyone know what this animal is? *(Show picture of the Dodo and accept ideas.)* I want you to copy this for me in a minute, but first I would like you to hear a little about this strange, unfamiliar animal.

It is a Dodo. It was a little bigger than a turkey and lived on the island of Mauritius. It was hunted by settlers and their dogs, and the last one was killed in 1681. Several museums in the world have remains, from which the picture has been drawn; but no living Dodo now exists.

This is not the only animal to be totally destroyed by mankind: over 100 species of animal have been completely wiped out. Those animals, specially created by God, have been totally destroyed by mankind; they will never ever exist again; they have vanished for ever from the earth. Can that be right?

TEXT:

God brought the animals to the man to see what he would name them;
and that is how they all got their names.   Genesis 2:19

PRACTICAL
ACTIVITY:

I would like you now to copy out the picture of the Dodo, then write down the number of animal species that Man has destroyed. Finally, make up a little prayer asking God to help us all to look after and be good stewards of the animals and birds placed in our care.

BIBLE SEARCH:

We have now spoken about the animals, let's look up texts to do with birds. Look up the following and write down what is happening:
Psalm 124:17
Leviticus 14:1–7
Song of Songs 2:12

LOOKING
FORWARD:

Let us read together the parable Jesus told which we find in the gospel of Luke 12:35–48.
How do you think that teaching of Jesus links with the work we have done today?

PSALM FOR
THE WEEK:

O LORD, our Lord,
your greatness is seen in all the world!
You appointed him ruler over everything you made;
you placed him over all creation:
sheep and cattle, and the wild animals too;
the birds and the fish
and the creatures in the seas.

O LORD, our Lord,
your greatness is seen in all the world! Psalm 8:1, 6–9

MEMORY
VERSE:

O Lord, our Lord,
your greatness is seen in all the world.

CLOSING
HYMN:

> Have you seen the pussy cat?   JP72
> If I were a butterfly   JP94
> Who put the colours in the rainbow?   JP288

The Serpent

AIM:	To help the children to understand how the first sin involved the whole of God's creation, animals and mankind together.
AIDS:	A black (or white) board, or large sheet of paper, to write on for all to see. Copies of the "string-man" (enlarged and duplicated on a photocopier). Sheets of A4 paper, roughly circular. Scissors; crayons, colouring pencils or felt-tip pens. A picture of a lamb.
PREPARATION:	None.
OPENING ACTIVITY:	Today we are going to have a class vote. I want to write on this board/sheet two lists. One of your favourite animals and the other of your least favourite. (*Accept animals, birds, etc. to make a list of six or eight; then a similar list, alongside, of the unpopular animals – spiders can be included!*)
	Now we are going to vote to find out the most popular and the least popular. You can only put your hand up once, for each list. Now hands up those who are voting for the first animal on our list. (*This activity may or may not show that snakes are unpopular. If it shows them to be unpopular the following parts flow more easily, but it is not necessary.*)
NEW WORDS:	Cursed – This means the opposite to a blessing. Being under a curse is an expression of God's disfavour.
	Disobedience – Not doing what you are told to do; the opposite of obedience.
PRESENTATION:	

(*Give out copies of the "string-man".*) Who can tell me what the picture you have in front of you is about. It is a copy of a Red Indian picture and shows that this Red Indian tribe realized how close to nature they, as humans, were. If you follow the line of the drawing everything is linked up, the man and all the animals, with one unbroken line.

Certain animals have become symbols for us. What do you think this stands for, or represents? (*Hold up a picture of a lamb, and ask what a lamb symbolizes.*) Yes, being innocent or sinless.

What about a dove? Yes, the sign of peace or the Holy Spirit. Can you think of any other animal that represents something else? How about the lion or the bulldog?

Let us now hear about the serpent in the garden of Eden: Genesis 3:1–5. Now can you tell me what the serpent stands for in the story? Yes, the power of evil.

Remember our "string-man"? What else do we notice about the story? The serpent tempts the woman, who takes the fruit and shares it with the man. They are all involved, each part of creation – the animal, the humans and the plant world. All fall into sin together.

TEXT: *Now the snake was the most cunning animal that*
the Lord God had made.   Genesis 3:1

PRACTICAL
ACTIVITY:
(The pieces of paper provided are to become snakes, so the children are instructed to decide on
"snake" colours and colour the paper accordingly.)
   Now with the scissors you have, and remembering
what we said about the "string-man" and God's plan that
all creation should be one, I want you to make a snake in
one and only one cutting of the paper, like this. *(Demon-*
strate, as shown.)

BIBLE SEARCH:
Let us look at two other places in the Bible where the
power of evil, the devil, is represented as a serpent.
Look up: Revelation 12:9
                Revelation 20:2

LOOKING
FORWARD:
Jesus came to put right the sin of the garden of Eden and restore wholeness to creation.
Look up and write out of the following:
   Mark 16:15 *(NIV)* – notice the words, "all creation".
   Romans 8:19–21 – "creation itself will be liberated".

PSALM FOR
THE WEEK:
LORD, you have made so many things!
   How wisely you made them all!
   The earth is filled with your creatures.
All of them depend on you
   to give them food when they need it.
When you turn away, they are afraid;
   when you take away their breath, they die
   and go back to the dust from which they came.
But when you give them breath, they are created;
   you give new life to the earth. Psalm 104:24, 27, 29–30

MEMORY
VERSE:
Lord, you have made so many things!
   How wisely you made them all!

CLOSING
HYMN:
> All things bright and beautiful   JP6/MP23
> God, whose farm is all creation   JP61
> Who put the colours in the rainbow?   JP288
> If I were a butterfly   JP94

41

Animals, Two by Two

AIM:	To help the children to understand that this is much more than a nice story. One animal, of the lowest kind, co-operated in the fall of mankind; two of every kind are to be part of the first promise of renewal, the new creation and covenant.
AIDS:	Copies of *Junior Praise* (Marshall Pickering) necessary to learn "Rise and Shine" (210).
PREPARATION:	Learn the actions that go with the song. The actions are too complicated to be explained here, but most church communities have young folk who could be invited in to teach these actions to the children.
OPENING ACTIVITY:	*(Either learn the song with the actions or, if this is not necessary, practise the song.)*
NEW WORDS:	*(Test the children on the words which are relevant to this session but which they have already learnt in previous lessons, for example Covenant, Stewardship.)*
PRESENTATION:	How well do you know the story of Noah and his ark? How many of each kind of animal did Noah take into the ark? No, you are wrong; it was not simply two of each animal. Listen now carefully to what the Bible says: Genesis 7:1–8, 19.

Did you notice? It was seven of every clean animal, that is animals like a cow or a sheep, but two of the unclean kind, like a camel or a rabbit. If you look up chapter 11 of Leviticus you will find the Jewish rules about clean and unclean animals.

Now let us read about what happened when Noah and all those animals were released from the ark: Genesis 9:1–17.

What I particularly want you to notice is the agreement between God and Noah, his family and all the animals. There is going to be a new beginning . . . God is going to protect mankind and the animal world, and promises that he will never again destroy the world with a flood. |
PRACTICAL ACTIVITY:	On the plain paper I have provided will you please draw and colour a picture of the scene *after* the flood, when Noah and his family step out onto dry land. Don't forget the rainbow. Then write along the bottom of your picture the words you will find in Genesis 9:16.
BIBLE SEARCH:	Look up and write out: Job 12:7–10 Isaiah 43:20–1
LOOKING FORWARD:	None.
PSALM FOR THE WEEK:	*To you, O LORD, I offer my prayer;* *in you, my God, I trust.* *Save me from the shame of defeat;* *don't let my enemies gloat over me!* *With faithfulness and love he leads* *all who keep his covenant and obey his commands.* Psalm 25:1–2, 10

TEXT: *"Take into the boat with you a male and a female of every kind of animal and of every kind of bird, in order to keep them alive."*　　　　Genesis 6:19

MEMORY
VERSE:
To you, O Lord, I offer my prayer.

Close this lesson with a short service for those who care for abused and neglected animals.

OPENING HYMN:　Rise and shine (with actions)　JP210
　　　　　　　　or If I were a butterfly　JP94
READING:　　Genesis 1:24–26 (followed by a few simple words on God entrusting animals to our care).
PRAYER:　　For all organizations and people who care for sick and neglected animals.
CLOSING HYMN:　Have you seen the pussy cat?　JP72
　　　　　　　　or Who put the colours in the rainbow?　JP288

LESSON 16:   *Dove of Hope and Peace*

AIM: To help the children to appreciate the virtue of hope, and the peace and tranquillity trust in God brings.

AIDS: None.

PREPARATION: Two volunteer pupils: one to dress up, before the session, in rainwear, waterproofs, etc.; one to dress up in summerwear, sunglasses, etc.

OPENING
ACTIVITY: *(Both dressed-up volunteers remain out of sight until called to appear before the others. Each comes out when called.)*

Today we are going to speak first of the weather. Tell me what weather our first volunteer is dressed for? *(Volunteer appears.)* Now what weather is our second volunteer expecting? What time of the year do you think is suggested by each of them? Now look at both and think: which type of weather do you like and enjoy most? Yes, the warm sunny weather.

When our wet-weather friend here is getting soaked, where is the sun? It is shining above the rain clouds. We have to wait for it to break through.

NEW WORDS: Hope – Believing that something good will happen.

Peace – Being happy, without anxiety and tension.

PRESENTATION: I want to ask each of you to complete a sentence for me. I am going to say, "I hope for . . ." and you have to finish the sentence. Every one must try and give a different answer. Here is an example: I say, "I hope for . . ." and you might answer, "hamburgers for dinner". Let's try it. Have you noticed that hope is to do with the future?

Next I want you all to imagine what it was like in Noah's ark, after over a month jammed together, with all those animals in the ark. Imagine the noise and the smell of all those animals. What do you think they were hoping for?

Can you imagine how happy everyone must have been when the dove returned with the olive branch? Their worries were over, the water was going down, they would be saved. So the dove with the olive branch became the symbol of hope and peace.

PRACTICAL
ACTIVITY: None.

BIBLE SEARCH: Look up the following texts, write them out and explain what you think the dove stands for in each text:
   Matthew 3:6
   Luke 3:22

LOOKING
FORWARD: Let's read together the first of those texts: Matthew 3:16. Jesus came up out of the water and at that moment the dove appeared to him. Can you see any connection with the story of Noah? Yes, when the waters receded, the dove brought the good news of salvation.

At home this week I want you to think about and write down your answer to this: "When in the Christian's life are the three – water, Holy Spirit and salvation – found

TEXT: *Noah sent out a dove to see if the water had gone down . . . he sent out the dove again . . . It returned to him in the evening, with a fresh olive leaf in its beak.* Genesis 8:8, 10–11

together in a very important Christian celebration?'' And, ''What *hope* does it give the Christian who is involved?''

PSALM FOR
THE WEEK:

Hear my prayer, O God;
don't turn away from my plea!
Listen to me and answer me;
I am worn out by my worries.
I am gripped by fear and trembling;
I am overcome with horror.
I wish I had wings, like a dove.
I would fly away and find rest.
I would quickly find myself a shelter
from the raging wind and the storm. Psalm 55:1–2, 5–6, 8

MEMORY
VERSE:

Hear my prayer, O God;
don't turn away from my plea.

CLOSING
HYMN:

> Have you heard the raindrops?   JP71
> All over the world the Spirit is moving   JP5
> I've got peace like a river   JP120
> Lord of all hopefulness   JP157
> You can't stop rain from falling down   JP297

LESSON 17: *Fed by Ravens*

AIM: To show the children that if, like Elijah, we trust in God and do what we sincerely believe is his will, he will provide for all our needs.

AIDS: A red folder, if possible, for the performance.

PREPARATION: To conduct a *This is Your Life* of Elijah, in imitation of the programme on television, the teacher/leader will have to read 1 Kings 17, 18 and 19; 2 Kings 1; 2 Kings 2:1–18. Then assign parts to capable pupils: Elijah, Elisha, widow of Zarepath, etc. The teacher and pupils will naturally need to rehearse the short (no longer than five minutes) performance.

OPENING
ACTIVITY: "Elijah: This is your Life."

(Conclude the interview with:) "And so, sir, what do you remember as your loneliest moment; the time when you felt most frightened and in need of God?" *(Answer – "Elijah" may read replies:)* "When I had to hide in the rocky ravine, near the Jordan, all by myself. I was frightened because there was nothing to eat, but I prayed and God sent me the ravens, who brought me food every day."

NEW WORDS: Divine providence:

Divine — To do with, or belonging to, God. So Divine help is help that comes from God.

Providence – God's foreseeing protection and care of his people, especially as a result of complete trust in God's loving care.

PRESENTATION: Let us now talk together about the story and your performance of "Elijah: This is your Life". Let's start with what you enjoyed about it . . . Can each of you now, in turn, tell me one thing that you learnt from it?

The new word we have learnt is "providence". Can anyone tell me what the connection is between that word and the story of the ravens bringing Elijah food?

What we have to remember is that "Elijah did what the Lord had told him"; he was obedient and trusted God completely. Notice that Elijah did not argue with God saying, "I can't go to that ravine, there will be nothing to do and nothing to eat." He just did what he was told; and God provided everything that he needed. There is a very important lesson for us in that story.

PRACTICAL
ACTIVITY: What I want you to do now, on the plain paper provided, is to explain simply the link between the word "providence" and the story of Elijah and the ravens; then draw a picture illustrating the story.

BIBLE SEARCH: What other references to birds are there in the Bible? We have, in previous lessons, learnt of the parts played by the raven and dove in the story of Noah and his family. Look up the following and write down the types of bird:

Luke 12:24   Matthew 10:29
Luke 2:24   Ezekiel 1:10
Matthew 24:28

TEXT:	*Elijah obeyed the LORD's command, and went and stayed by the brook of Cherith. He drank water from the brook, and ravens brought him bread and meat every morning and every evening.* 1 Kings 17:5–6

LOOKING FORWARD:

In his preaching Jesus refers constantly to nature and examples from life in the countryside. Birds are frequently mentioned, and that is not surprising because the wide fertile valley of the Jordan that runs the whole length of Jesus' country was the route in the autumn and spring of thousands of migrating birds. In the autumn birds from the north travelled down the valley seeking the warmth of North Africa for the winter. In the spring, Jesus and his friends would see the flocks of migrating birds return up the Jordan valley.

Jesus told us that God the Father knows and cares about all those birds, and if he cares about sparrows, won't he care about us, too?

"Not one sparrow falls to the ground without your Father's consent. . . . So do not be afraid; you are worth much more than many sparrows." *(Matthew 10:29, 31.)*

PSALM FOR THE WEEK:

But I am like an olive-tree growing in the house of God;
I trust in his constant love for ever and ever.
I will always thank you, God, for what you have done;
in the presence of your people
I will proclaim that you are good. Psalm 52:8–9

MEMORY VERSE:

I trust in his constant love
for ever and ever.

CLOSING HYMN:

Father I place into your hands   JP42/MP133
Be still and know that I am God   JP22/MP48
Will your anchor hold in the storms of life?   JP290/MP275

The Talking Donkey

AIM: To show the children that God intended that there should be a partnership between humans and animals; the animals are not just to be used but deserve our respect and loyalty.

AIDS: Three willing and able readers are required.

PREPARATION: Research and find addresses of associations, societies and organizations that promote animal welfare and rights; for example a local donkey sanctuary or, in the UK, the RSPCA.

OPENING ACTIVITY: *(The leader must first read the story of Balaam's donkey, Numbers 22:21–38, prefacing it with the following:)*

This is an interesting story which is a little hard to understand at first hearing. Balaam was not a Jew; he was a wise man who was believed to have powers to bless or curse. A king, who feared the Jewish people, wanted Balaam to curse the Jews. God told him to go, but to bless and not curse them.

Before we hear three stories taken from newspapers, I would like to point out that the donkey in the story we have just heard was completely faithful and loyal to his master. As the angel said, the donkey's action saved Balaam's life. Let's hear three similar stories from everyday life.

Reader A: Eight-year-old Wayne Norgate prayed for a miracle as he was swept out to sea in a rubber dinghy. With his father unable to swim to the rescue because of the strong current, Wayne sat sobbing as the flimsy craft was buffeted by the waves. "I just prayed to God for help," he said, "then I felt something under the water nudging the boat. When I looked down I saw the seal." The seal edged Wayne toward the safety of shallow water near the beach, where he was picked up by a boat.

Reader B: A twelve stone dog used his weight and his head when his mistress was attacked by a mugger. Blue, a two-year-old rottweiller, could not bite the man because he was muzzled, so he hurled himself at the attacker and knocked him over. Dazed and bleeding, the man picked himself up and fled. Mother of two, Valerie Mansbridge, said last night, "I dread to think what would have happened if Blue had not been there. He deserves a medal."

Reader C: Teenager Adam Maguire told last night how a school of friendly dolphins saved him from a shark. "It attacked me twice, and I was too exhausted to fight as it came a third time," said the seventeen-year-old Australian, who had been out surfing. "Then the dolphins swam at the shark and knocked it away. They definitely saved my life. I wouldn't be here today if it wasn't for them." Adam, in hospital in New South Wales, pulled back his pyjamas to show bandages covering the 300cm wound caused by the shark's teeth.

Presenter: There are many stories of animals, birds and, as we have just heard, fish coming to the rescue of a human being. Balaam's donkey tried to warn him and he did not understand.

TEXT:	*The angel said, "Your donkey saw me and turned aside three times. If it hadn't, I would have killed you and spared the donkey."* <div align="right">Numbers 22:33</div>

NEW WORD:	Gentile – Balaam was a Gentile, that is he was not a Jew. So everyone who is not a Jew is a Gentile.
PRESENTATION:	This story is an interesting one because in it we can see how God uses anyone, or anything he likes, to get something done. In the story, God's chosen people are in the background. God uses a spirit, an angel, to convey a message; he uses an animal, a donkey too; and the person who is to do his will is not even a member of his chosen people. God can use *who* he wills, *when* he wills.
PRACTICAL ACTIVITY:	Now today I want us to do something quite different. I am going to share the addresses of animal welfare groups and we are going to write letters to them and ask them to send us information about their work. We will first draft out our letters in rough (*help will be necessary for the younger ones*) before we write out the letters to send.
BIBLE SEARCH:	Look up 2 Peter 2:15–16 and decide (with help) what it is about. Look up 2 Peter 2:1 for a clue.
LOOKING FORWARD:	Look up Matthew 21:5 to find out who also rode a donkey. Look up Zechariah 9:9 to see where it had been foretold.

PSALM FOR THE WEEK:	*Remind me each morning of your constant love,*
	   for I put my trust in you.
	My prayers go up to you;
	   show me the way I should go.
	
	I go to you for protection, LORD;
	   rescue me from my enemies.
	You are my God;
	   teach me to do your will.
	Be good to me, and guide me on a safe path. Psalm 143:8–10

MEMORY VERSE:	*You are my God;* *teach me to do your will.*
CLOSING HYMN:	Have you seen the pussy cat, sitting on the wall? JP72 Who put the colours in the rainbow? JP288 He's got the whole world in His hands JP78

LESSON 19: *The Wolf and the Lamb*

AIM: To explore with the children the gift of peace, especially in relation to the coming of Christ.

AIDS: A bag or box of sweets. A clear area where children can sit, perhaps on the floor, in a large circle. Two cards, one with the word "lamb" on it, the other with the word "wolf". A redundant white sheet, to tear or cut into a banner shape; also felt-tip pens.

PREPARATION: Keep the children outside the place where they are usually taught, lined up in silence. Observe the group and decide on a criterion (preferably something that they are wearing).

OPENING ACTIVITY: *(As each child passes the leader/teacher s/he is given one of two instructions: either to form part of a large, outer circle; or take a sweet from a box or bag held by the teacher and sit as part of a small, inner circle. The criterion of choice for the latter small group could be that the children were all wearing something blue or red. The criterion must be random and not obvious to the children.)*

(The inner group sit and eat their sweets-conscious, in a self-satisfied way, that they are privileged, while complaints start to arise from the outer, larger group. "It's not fair" will soon be heard. At this point the teacher/leader leads a discussion.)

What is the matter? What is unfair? How do you feel about this? Do you feel friendly towards the inner group? Do you feel full of peace and happiness?

(Teacher/leader reveals the criterion of choice and hands an equal number of sweets to the members of the outer group. All go to their usual places.)

NEW WORDS: Peace – What is peace? *(Accept suggestions and if possible write these down on a public board. Draw the suggestions together to form a definition which the children are asked to copy out.)*

Messiah – The Hebrew word for "Christ". They both mean, "the annointed one" and refer to the promised saviour that the Jewish people believed would come to lead God's people.

PRESENTATION: Hands up those who were in the outer circle. I am going to hold up two cards, one after the other, and ask you which animal did you feel most like when you sat in the outer circle. *(Hold up a card with the word "lamb" then a card with the word "wolf".)*

Hands up those who felt more like a wolf than a lamb. *(The majority of hands should be up.)* Why did you feel more like a wolf than a lamb? Yes, because you felt it was unfair.

The prophet Isaiah said that when the Messiah comes there will be fairness and peace; the wolf and lamb will live together and the leopard will lie down with the goat. But only, of course, if people accepted that Jesus was the Messiah and placed their complete trust in him.

PRACTICAL ACTIVITY: We are going to spread the white sheet on the ground and turn it into a banner that we can put up in the church. In the centre we will have the words:

THE LORD BLESSES HIS PEOPLE WITH PEACE

and around the edge we will all add pictures, perhaps of the wolf and lamb lying down together, or any picture that suggests Peace.

TEXT:	*Wolves and sheep will live together in peace,*
	    and leopards will lie down with young goats.
	                                                      Isaiah 11:6

BIBLE SEARCH:	Look up the following references and write down what the Bible says about Peace:
	    Isaiah 48:18
	    Isaiah 32:17
	    Job 3:26
	    Galatians 5:22

LOOKING FORWARD:	The prophet Isaiah foretold that when the Christ came he would be the "Prince of Peace" *(Isaiah 9:6).* Look up what the angels sang at his birth: Luke 2:14. Write out the words of the Prince of Peace, which you will find in John 14:27.

PSALM FOR THE WEEK:	*The LORD rules over the deep waters;*
	    he rules as king for ever.
	The LORD gives strength to his people
	    and blesses them with peace. Psalm 29:10–11

MEMORY VERSE:	*The Lord blesses his people with peace.*
CLOSING HYMN:	I've got peace like a river JP120/MP114 Peace I give to you JP196 Make me a channel of your peace JP161/MP153

The Lost Sheep

AIM:	To remind the children of God's loving concern for the sinner; and the mission of Christ Jesus to seek out those who have gone astray.
AIDS:	A small object to be "lost" and "found" (this could be a knitted or stuffed toy lamb, but any object will do).
PREPARATION:	Before the children enter the room the object is hidden. Do not make it too easy, otherwise the activity is over too quickly.
OPENING ACTIVITY:	*(Outside the room the children are told of the "lost" object and asked to find it. They are then let in, the youngest first.)*

OPENING ACTIVITY continued:

Now you have found what was hidden, and we pretended was lost, let's read our Bible text for today: Ezekiel 34:7–12.

That text is from the Old Testament. Can anyone think of anything like it in the New Testament? Yes, Jesus declares that he is the Good Shepherd who cares for his flock.

Has anyone here ever been lost? *(Listen to any stories.)* I now want you all to imagine that you are either the object that was found in this room, or a lost sheep. Can you imagine what it would be like? How would you feel when you found that you were completely on your own, with no one else around? Would anyone volunteer to share their feelings as the lost sheep?

NEW WORDS:

Mission – This word comes from a Latin word which means "to send"; so someone who has or is on a mission, is sent. Jesus Christ had a mission: he was sent by God the Father.

Missionaries are people who are sent out by the Christian community to spread the Good News of Jesus.

PRESENTATION:

Can anyone tell me what happens in your family if your mother or father loses the car keys or a purse? What will happen if the keys are not found? Is it really important to try hard to find them? Isn't it true that the more important a lost thing is, the more effort goes into trying to find it?

God believes that a person who has turned his or her back on him is so valuable that he, himself, will go looking for ways of bringing that person back. That does not mean that God will force the person to return.

In the following story, told by Jesus, the father in the story stands for God. Notice how the father behaves. The Parable of the Lost Son: Luke 15:11–24.

Did you notice how the father ran to meet his son? That is how God looks out for the return of the sinner.

PRACTICAL ACTIVITY:

(Put the children into appropriate sized groups.) Now in your groups I want you to –

1. Talk about a modern example of the lost son or lost sheep. For example, on a school trip the teacher finds, at the railway station or as the party get on the coach, that one of the children is missing. She leaves the others while she goes looking for the lost pupil.

"I, the Sovereign LORD, tell you that I myself will look for my sheep and take care of them."   Ezekiel 34:11

2.   Make up a little play, taking care to give parts to everyone in the group, to show us the example you have thought of.

(Plays are presented to the class.)

BIBLE SEARCH
AND LOOKING
FORWARD:

Jesus told several stories about searching out the sinner. Look up Luke 15:1–7 and Luke 15:8–10.
　　Which of those stories links with the following texts?
　　John 10:11
　　John 10:14
　　1 Peter 5:4

PSALM FOR
THE WEEK:

The LORD is my shepherd;
*　I have everything I need.*
He lets me rest in fields of green grass
*　and leads me to quiet pools of fresh water.*
He gives me new strength.
He guides me in the right paths,
*　as he has promised.*   Psalm 23:1–3

MEMORY
VERSE:

The Lord is my shepherd;
*　I have everything I need.*

CLOSING
HYMN:

> The Lord's my Shepherd, I'll not want   JP243/MP227 also JP241 or JP244
> Put your hand in the hand of the man who stilled the water JP206
> When the road is rough and steep   JP279
> "Follow me" says Jesus   JP46

LESSON 21: *On Eagle's Wings*

AIM: To help the children to understand that just as the power of God brought the people of God out of the slavery of Egypt, so that same power can free us and keep us close to him.

AIDS: Pictures of various animals, including a picture of an eagle in flight. A good reader to read the story.

PREPARATION: Divide the children into four equal groups, mixing ages and abilities, so that they can assist one another in the Practical activity. A group must not have less than three pupils. If numbers are low, or the children rather young, do not use Revelation.

OPENING
ACTIVITY:
(Show the pictures one at a time, and ask the children what quality they associate with each animal.
For example: Timid as a mouse
*   Cheeky as a sparrow*
*   Friendly as a dog, etc.*
What quality do they associate with the eagle?
Power? Strength? Majesty?)

Reader: This is the story of a mother eagle that had built her nest on a ledge of rock jutting precariously over a steep and dangerous precipice. Soaring through the air one day, returning to her nest, she was startled by what she saw. Clinging desperately to the jagged edge of a rock at the top of the canyon was her baby eagle, struggling with all its might to prevent a fall, more than a thousand feet below, that was sure to crush its body. The baby fell.

Unable to get to the ledge before her little one fell, the mother eagle, with the speed of lightning, swooped low beneath the jutting rock, spread her strong wings to break the fall of her darling, and with her precious cargo clinging to the feathers of her mighty wings glided safely to the canyon's floor. *(Anon.)*

NEW WORD: Liberation – Freedom; to be free of something that constricts and holds us back.

PRESENTATION: None.

PRACTICAL
ACTIVITY:
(One of the following Bible texts is given to each of the groups and together they are to:
– Find the text and read its setting.
– Agree together what it says about God and his people.
– Choose someone in the group to tell the whole class about the group's findings.)

BIBLE SEARCH: Deuteronomy 32:10–12   Exodus 19:3–6
Isaiah 40:29–31   Revelation 12:14

LOOKING
FORWARD:
None.

PSALM FOR
THE WEEK:
(Having copied out the psalm below, the groups are asked to sit facing one another, two of the groups facing the other two. One "side" reads out the verses and the other the refrain, which comes between the verses. Start with all reading A, the refrain.)

TEXT: *The LORD called to Moses from the mountain and told him*
to say to the Israelites, Jacob's descendants: "You saw what I, the LORD,
did to the Egyptians and how I carried you as an eagle carries her young on her
wings, and brought you here to me."   Exodus 19:3–4

A: *Refrain:*
    He will raise you up on eagle's wings,
        bear you on the breath of dawn,
    make you to shine like the sun,
        and hold you in the palm of his hand.

B: *Whoever goes to the LORD for safety,*
        whoever remains under the protection of the Almighty,
    can say to him,
        "You are my defender and protector.
        You are my God; in you I trust."

A: *Refrain.*

B: *He will keep you safe from all hidden dangers*
        and from all deadly diseases.
    He will cover you with his wings;
        you will be safe in his care;
        his faithfulness will protect and defend you.

A: *Refrain.*

B: *You need not fear any dangers at night*
        or sudden attacks during the day
        or the plagues that strike in the dark
        or the evils that kill in daylight.

A: *Refrain.*
                                        Psalm 91:1–6

MEMORY   *"You are my defender and protector.*
VERSE: *You are my God; in you I trust."*

CLOSING
HYMN:

> My God is so big, so strong and so mighty   JP169
> Be bold, Be strong, for the Lord your God is with you   JP14
> Be still and know that I am God   JP22/MP16
> God who made the earth   JP63

55

LESSON 22: # Inside the Great Fish

AIM:	To help the children to appreciate that God gives us many opportunities to serve him; and we must learn to recognize those opportunities and not fail our loving Father.
AIDS:	The children should have their bibles with them. Required for each pupil: a sheet of plain A4 paper; a piece of tissue paper approximately 8in × 4in; a piece of cardboard; scissors and glue.
PREPARATION:	Acquire the use of a version of the Bible which is set out for part reading, e.g. *The Dramatised Bible* (Marshall Pickering). Alternatively the teacher/leader may divide the text of Jonah 1–3 into parts.
OPENING ACTIVITY:	What fruit did Adam and Eve eat in the garden of Eden? *(Wait for answer.)*

What kind of fish swallowed Jonah?

How did Mary and Joseph get to Bethlehem?

(The children will give these answers: 1. apple; 2. whale; 3. donkey.)
Those answers aren't strictly true. Let's look up the correct answers:
  Genesis 3:1–13
  Jonah 1:17
  Luke 2:4–7
So the correct answers are: 1. the fruit
  2. a big fish
  3. no mention of transport.
It was probably the mystery plays of medieval Europe which suggested that Adam and Eve took an apple and Mary travelled by donkey to Bethlehem; and early translators of the Bible who suggested that Jonah was swallowed by a whale. When we read and study God's word we must be accurate, we must not add what is not there.

NEW WORD:	Opportunity – *(Ask an older child to explain to the younger or less able children what the word means, giving examples from family life.)*
PRESENTATION:	The story of Jonah is not very long and full of action so we will listen to it being read in full.

Jonah was asked to do something for God. He was given an opportunity to serve the Lord, but tried to run away and dodge the opportunity. You heard what happened. The lesson to us is clear: when we have the opportunity of serving God we must not run away.

PRACTICAL ACTIVITY:	Jonah was asked to go to Nineveh, which would have been a long journey of about 500 miles overland, a dry and dusty journey. He decided to go by ship, a rough and wet journey, to Tarshish in Spain, over 1500 miles away.

We are now going to have a race, but first you have to cut your piece of tissue paper into the shape of a big fish.

Now in teams of four, on the floor, we are going to race our fish to Tarshish. You "blow" your fish along by waving the card behind it.

TEXT:	*At the LORD's command a large fish swallowed Jonah,* *and he was inside the fish for three days and nights.* <div align="right">Jonah 1:17</div>

(When the race is over the children draw a man, Jonah, in the middle of their sheet of A4 paper, then stick the fish shape over the top. This should be done to allow room underneath to write a short, two-line prayer: "Lord, may we never run away from the opportunity of doing your will.")

BIBLE SEARCH:	One of the favourite themes of the apostle Paul was making the most of God-given opportunities. Find the following and write out what Paul says about using such opportunities:
	    Colossians 4:5
	    Galatians 6:9–10
	    Ephesians 5:15–16

LOOKING FORWARD:	Jonah was inside the fish for three days and three nights. He was in the dark and would have been thought to have "died". On the third day he came out alive. Jesus rose to life on the third day. Let's look at Matthew 12:38–45: *Jesus said . . . "In the same way that Jonah spent three days and nights in the big fish, so will the Son of Man spend three days and nights in the depths of the earth."*

PSALM FOR THE WEEK:	In the belly of the great fish Jonah prayed a "psalm" of thanksgiving:
	
	"In my distress, O LORD, I called to you,
	    and you answered me.
	From deep in the world of the dead
	    I cried for help and you heard me.
	
	Those who worship worthless idols
	    have abandoned their loyalty to you.
	But I will sing praises to you;
	    I will offer you a sacrifice
	    and do what I have promised.
	Salvation comes from the LORD!" Jonah 2:2, 8–9

MEMORY VERSE:	*"In my distress, Lord, I called to you,* *and you answered me."*

CLOSING HYMN:	<table><tr><td>Come listen to my tale JP30 You can't stop rain from falling down JP297 Do you want a Pilot? JP40</td></tr></table>

LESSON 23: *In the Lions' Den*

AIM: To encourage the children to persevere in their Christian faith, whatever difficulties and temptations they face in the future.

AIDS: For Handprint Lions: One large sheet of paper; one thick felt-tip pen; three bowls of thick hand paint (mix food colouring with wallpaper paste, without fungicide) – brown, orange and yellow. For wallpaper panels: A length of approximately two metres of redundant wallpaper; a selection of thick felt-tip pens.

PREPARATION: Prepare and rehearse a small group of seven children to act out the story of Daniel. The players will comprise: Daniel, three satraps, King Darius and two soldiers (to arrest Daniel and throw him into the lions' den). While parts could be written, most children, once they are familiar with the story, can produce a play without a script.

OPENING ACTIVITY: The play, *Daniel in the Lions' Den*.
Did you notice why Daniel was thrown to the lions? It was because he believed in the one true God and would not give up praising and worshipping him. The people among whom he lived believed in many gods.
(An alternative opening activity, particularly suitable if the age range is young, is Handprint Lions. Help the children to draw a lion's head on the large sheet of paper. Then ask the children to take turns in printing their hands round the lion's head. Their prints form the lion's mane. If it is a large group then several lions can be made, and Daniel added for a frieze in the church. BEWARE: Vigilance is required, otherwise handprints will go everywhere!)

NEW WORD: Monotheism – This unfamiliar word means belief in only one God. So Christians, Jews and Moslems are all monotheists. Daniel, as a good Jew, was a monotheist; the people among whom he lived were polytheists (belief in many gods).

PRESENTATION: Daniel would not give up his belief in the one true God and was thrown to the lions to be eaten. But God preserved him. The first Christians suffered for their beliefs, and some of them were fed to lions, too.
Listen to what Tacitus, the Roman historian, wrote in 116 AD about what happened to the Christians in the first Roman persecution in 64AD. Tacitus is explaining that the Emperor Nero, who set fire to the city of Rome, arrested the Christians and blamed them for the fire.

TEXT:	*So the king gave orders for Daniel to be arrested and he was thrown into the pit filled with lions.* Daniel 6:16

Nero punished with the utmost refinement of cruelty a class of people hated for their abominations, called Christians. Accordingly arrest was first made of those who confessed to being Christians. Besides being put to death they were made to serve as objects of amusement; they were clad in the hides of beasts and torn to death by dogs; others were crucified, others set on fire.

Jesus had prophesied, "If they persecuted me, they will persecute you too" *(John 15:20)*. Throughout the history of the Christian church, nearly 2,000 years, there has hardly been a time when Christians have not been prepared to suffer like Daniel and those early Christians.

PRACTICAL ACTIVITY:	*(Wallpaper Panels: Lay the length of wallpaper, plain side up, on the floor; divide it into three equal panels. Invite the children to work on one of the three panels. It might be easier to cut the panels apart for the work and re-unite the parts when the work is complete.)*
	(The first panel is to depict Daniel in the lions' den; the second, the sufferings of the early Christians; and the third (requiring thought and guidance) how Christians suffer today for their faith.)
BIBLE SEARCH:	Look up and write out the following texts to learn how Christians should behave when persecuted:
	Matthew 5:44–45a Romans 12:14
	1 Corinthians 4:12 Acts 7:59–60
LOOKING FORWARD:	None.
PSALM FOR THE WEEK:	*I am worn out, LORD, waiting for you to save me;*
	* I place my trust in your word.*
	Your commandments are all trustworthy;
	* men persecute me with lies – help me!*
	Because of your constant love be good to me,
	* so that I may obey your laws.*
	Psalm 119:81, 86, 88
MEMORY VERSE:	*Because of your constant love be good to me.*

CLOSING HYMN:	Your hand, O God, has guided JP298
	We shall overcome JP270
	One more step along the world I go JP188
	Daniel was a man of prayer JP36

LESSON 24:   *The King's Donkey*

AIM: To help the pupils to understand and appreciate that just as the crowd that day outside Jerusalem acknowledged Jesus as Lord and Christ, so can we every day.

AIDS: The children should have their bibles to hand. For the Palm Sunday presentation, branches of greenery for all those in the "crowd".

PREPARATION: A dramatic presentation is the best method to teach *The King's Donkey* and Palm Sunday. The number of children available for the "crowd" will dictate how many branches of "palm" (any branch from most trees will do) are required. Each member of the crowd needs a "chant" from the gospels, e.g. "Hosanna", "Blessed is the King who comes in the name of the Lord". Try to use all the phrases in the gospels.

Decide who will play Jesus, and two or three of his apostles (these can be dispensed with if short of numbers).

The biggest problem is the donkey. A small "Jesus" riding on a big boy's back, who is on all fours, is one solution; a real donkey is wonderful and can be possible with proper and early planning. Involve the children in the planning and they will often come up with a solution that will not occur to adults.

For success, the crowd must appreciate that they can be as noisy as they like, shouting their phrases and waving their branches. If it goes well the youngsters may be invited to repeat their performance for the church on Palm Sunday.

OPENING ACTIVITY: Let's look up the events of the first Palm Sunday and discover the differences in the four accounts:

Matthew 21:1–11   Mark 11:1–11
John 12:12–16   Luke 19:28–40

(Teacher/leader can help to list the differences, perhaps on a public chart or board. For example, John only speaks of a donkey, whereas Matthew says the donkey has her colt with her. And Mark and Luke only speak of a colt. What the people in the crowd shout out is a little different in each gospel.)

(When this is complete all should find Zechariah 9:9–10. This should be read, with authority, by the teacher/leader.)

NEW WORD: Messianic – We learnt the meaning of the word "Messiah" a few lessons ago. Let us see who can still remember its meaning.

"Messianic" means, to belong to the Messiah, or Christ. So "Messianic titles" are names or titles given to the coming Messiah.

PRESENTATION: In our opening activity we discovered that each of the gospel writers has slight differences about two principal points: First, whether there was a donkey used or a donkey and a colt. Second, the words shouted out by the crowd were a little different.

Do these differences mean that the gospel writers are not telling the truth or have remembered what happened wrongly? No, certainly not; the differences give strength to the story.

If four of you had been there, in the crowd, that day, and now told us all what happened we would get four slightly different accounts. One of you would say, "Where I

TEXT:

The disciples brought the donkey and the colt,
threw their cloaks over them, and Jesus got on.
Matthew 21:7

---

was in the crowd they were shouting 'Hosanna to the Son of David'" (Matthew's gospel). Another one of you would say, "Where I was in the crowd they were shouting 'Blessed is the king who comes in the name of the Lord'" (Luke's gospel). Again another could say, "They were shouting 'Blessed is the King of Israel' (John's gospel) where I was."

The important point is that the crowd were all greeting Jesus as the promised Messiah; they used Messianic titles specially reserved for the coming Messiah. For example, "Son of David" and "King of Israel".

One donkey or a donkey and her colt? That is the next difference we discovered. The answer is in the prophecy from Zechariah that I read out to you. You will remember that two of the gospel writers, Matthew and John, quote it. This was a Messianic prophecy about the coming of the promised Messiah and the two gospel writers wanted to remind their readers of this and that, just as foretold, there was a donkey and a colt.

However Luke and Mark want us to concentrate on the fact that it was a young donkey (a colt) and not a horse. It is the *type* of Messiah who comes that Luke and Mark want us to think about; a Messiah who comes gently, humbly and in peace.

The Jews of Jesus' time wanted a warrior Messiah who would ride into Jerusalem on a great war horse, to drive out the hated Romans. Our King is a king of peace.

PRACTICAL
ACTIVITY:

The King's Donkey. (It must be remembered that this is not a static "play" but a noisy procession from one place to another; from the hall into the church? On "arrival" (wherever the procession is destined), it can be concluded with a praise hymn and a prayer.)

BIBLE SEARCH: None.

LOOKING
FORWARD: None.

PSALM FOR
THE WEEK:

Save us, LORD, save us!
  Give us success, O LORD!

May God bless the one who comes
    in the name of the LORD!
  From the Temple of the LORD we bless you.
The LORD is God; he has been good to us.
With branches in your hands, start the festival
    and march round the altar.
Save us, LORD, save us!
  Give us success, O LORD! Psalm 118:25–27, 29

MEMORY
VERSE:

May God bless the one who comes in the name of
    the Lord!

CLOSING
HYMN:

(or hymns for the end of the procession)

Clap your hands all you people   JP26
Children of Jerusalem   JP24
Come and praise the Lord our King (chorus and verses 5&6) JP34
Hallelu, hallelu, hallelu, hallelujah   JP67
Praise to the Lord our God, let us sing together   JP205
We have a King who rides a donkey   JP264

Term Three

THE DISCIPLES OF JESUS

LESSON 25:   *The Twelve*

AIM:
To help the children to understand and appreciate the important role of the twelve apostles as the foundation stones of the Christian Church.

AIDS:
A small bundle of sticks, a couple of house bricks and a few strands of straw.

PREPARATION:
Arrange for one or more of the children to be sent on a short errand (but do not inform the children concerned until the moment they are sent); it could be to collect a sheet of music for the pianist or something similar. Borrow a number of hard hats or helmets from a local builder or building site for the children to put on; or, ask a builder, architect or construction worker to appear during the Presentation, wearing a hard hat (s/he may be a member of the church congregation), and say a few words (only a few) about their work. Conclude with a few words on the importance of deep and strong foundations for buildings.

OPENING
ACTIVITY:
I want to start by sending *(name)* on an errand for me. *(Give directions.)* While s/he/they are gone let us look at the text.

Can anyone suggest why Jesus wanted to keep the twelve friends near him? It says, "so that they might be with him". Why? Yes, so that they could learn.

Years ago when there were crafts and trades men who were skilled at their trade, like a printer or a carpenter or a blacksmith, would have young lads as apprentices. The tradesman would keep the young man close to him for a number of years, until he learnt the trade. Then the young man would be sent out as a journeyman, to do jobs – like repair work – on his own, away from the workshop. Eventually, he would be accepted as a craftsman in his own right.

That's similar to what Jesus was doing; he taught his apostles and then sent them out. *(Assuming the errand boy/girl has returned)* I sent *(name)* to do something for me; s/he was like an apostle, because the word in Greek for "to send" is *apostello*. Apostles are those who are sent. Jesus sent his twelve special disciples to spread the Good News.

NEW WORDS:
Let us write about the word we have learnt.

Apostle – It is used to describe those who were "sent out" by Christ; not all the disciples, but those who had received a special commission (or sending) from the Lord; the Twelve and Paul, who claimed that he too had been sent by Christ.

Apostolic – Belonging to the apostles or coming from the apostles; so one of the marks of the Church is that it is "Apostolic", built upon the faith and teaching of the Twelve.

PRESENTATION:
How many of you know the story of the three little pigs? The first wanted to build his house of straw *(show the straw)*; the second decided to use sticks *(show the sticks)*; and the third chose bricks *(show the bricks)*.

Who can tell us what happened to the one who used straw? And who will tell us about the fate of the pig who used sticks? You know that the wolf could not blow down the house of bricks; why?

TEXT:	*Jesus chose twelve, whom he named apostles. "I have chosen you to be with me," he told them. "I will also send you out to preach."*
	Mark 3:14

(Introduce the "builder" or give out the hard hats and ask the children which item they, as builders, would use for the foundations of a building.) Jesus chose "bricks" or rather "stones" as the foundation of his Christian community: the apostles.

Let's do our Bible search now, together.

BIBLE SEARCH: Let us together find Ephesians 2:20–22 and read it out.

We, the Church, are built upon the foundation stones – the apostles and early Christian teachers (prophets) – with Jesus as the chief cornerstone.

Let us now find Matthew 16:13–18. The apostle Simon, son of Jonah, speaks up for all the apostles and Jesus says, "Peter, you are a rock, and on this rock foundation I will build my church."

Now go to Revelation 21:14: "The city's wall was built on twelve foundation-stones, on which were written the names of the twelve apostles of the Lamb."

To finish please look up Matthew 10:1–4 and write out the list of the Twelve.

PRACTICAL
ACTIVITY: Hundreds of years ago symbols or emblems were used for the apostles. Let's draw a few of these. First the apostle Andrew, who is the patron of Scotland, and also Russia.

The apostle Andrew
patron of Scotland
and Russia

The apostle Thomas
patron of Builders

Now the apostle Thomas is the patron of builders, because a tradition in east India, where he is believed to have gone to preach the Gospel, has it that he built a church there with his own hands.

LOOKING
BACKWARD: Why did Jesus chose twelve disciples as his apostles? Why not ten or seven or fourteen? The answer is in the Old Testament. Find Genesis 35:22–26, then Genesis 49:28.

The Jewish people, the first people of God, were founded on the twelve tribes of Israel. The Christian Church, the new people of God, was founded on the twelve apostles.

PSALM FOR
THE WEEK: *Sing a new song to the LORD;*
he has doe wonderful things!
By his own power and holy strength
he has won the victory.
The LORD announced his victory;
he made his saving power known to the nations.

65

He kept his promise to the people of Israel
with loyalty and constant love for them.
All people everywhere have seen the victory of our God. Psalm 98:1–3

MEMORY
VERSE:

Sing a new song to the Lord;
he has done wonderful things.

CLOSING
HYMN:

Put your hand in the hand   JP266
I want to walk with Jesus   JP124
I sing a song of the saints of God   JP115

The Family of Bethany

AIM: To show that Jesus had ordinary family friends who were dear to him.

AIDS: Sufficient simple maps of the Holy Land for one between three children (the Israel Tourist Office will happily supply such). A copy of the picture below of a house at the time of Jesus. Put the children into groups of three. Give each group three pieces of paper and at least one Bible.

PREPARATION: None.

OPENING ACTIVITY:

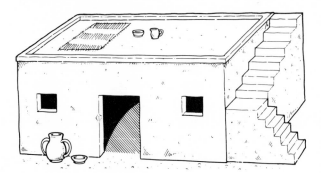

Using the maps, find Bethany, then answer these questions: What is the name of the big city near Bethany where Martha and Mary might have gone shopping? *(Jerusalem.)* Why would Lazarus not go fishing in the sea which was about twelve miles away? *(Dead Sea, nothing living in it.)* Look up Joshua 6 and then find the city spoken of there on the map. How far was it from Lazarus' and his sisters' home?

Here is the type of house the family at Bethany lived in. Try drawing a copy of it.

NEW WORDS: *(In modern society it is not safe to assume that all the children will have a clear picture of what Christians traditionally understand by the word "family". If appropriate explain and give a simple definition to copy out.)*

Nuclear family – A family which only includes the mother, the father and a child or children.

Extended family – When "family" is understood as including parents, children, grandparents, aunts, uncles, etc.

PRESENTATION: Can anyone see any connection bethween our groups and the word "family"? Yes, many families consist of three: mother, father and child. Two people, a couple, are not a family; a couple become a family when a child is born. So when Joseph and Mary took baby Jesus home to Nazareth they were a family.

However, a family can remain a family when the parents die and, for example, brothers and sisters continue to live together.

Each of you, in the groups, have a sheet of paper. Decide who, in your group, is to be Martha, Mary and Lazarus.

If you are Martha, look up Luke 10:38–42 and John 11:1–44, and find out as much as you can about her.

TEXT:	*Lazarus lived in Bethany, the town where Mary and her sister Martha lived . . . Jesus loved Martha and her sister and Lazarus.* John 11:1–5

If you are Mary look up Luke 10:38–42, John 11 and John 12:1–8.

If you are Lazarus look up John 11:1–44 and John 12:9–19.

PRACTICAL
ACTIVITY:

Now that you have found out about your "character", prepare for us all to see a little play about one incident in the lives of Martha, Mary and Lazarus. This could be imaginary: for example, show what happened in the Bethany home when news of Jesus' death arrived; or news of his resurrection.

BIBLE SEARCH:

(If, after the above, it is still desired.)
What did these families do?
    Acts 10:1–2, 24–48
    Acts 16:33

LOOKING
BACKWARD:

The idea of "family" is very important in the Bible. Starting from the first couple and the family of Noah (Genesis 7), God uses the family life of Abraham and Sarah (Genesis 18), Isaac and Rebekah (Genesis 27) and many others, until God himself comes among us and lives as the member of a family in a small, unimportant Galilean town called Nazareth (Luke 2:51).

PSALM FOR
THE WEEK:

God, be merciful to us and bless us;
  look on us with kindness,
so that the whole world may know your will;
  so that all nations may know your salvation.
May the peoples praise you, O God;
  may all the peoples praise you!
May the nations be glad and sing for joy.
                  Psalm 67:1–4

MEMORY
VERSE:

May the peoples praise you, O God;
  may all the peoples praise you!

CLOSING
HYMN:

Bind us together, Lord   JP17
Father, I place into your hands   JP42
He's got the whole world in his hands   JP78

Mary of Magdala

AIM:

To help the children to appreciate the great importance of what Mary witnessed at the tomb and the centrality of the resurrection.

AIDS:

Print clearly the following words, and any similar ones, on pieces of card or paper. Produce two complete sets of cards. One set is hidden, before the session, around the room/church/hall, etc.

First day of week	Sunday
Tomb	Grave
Mary of Magdala	Mary Magdalene
Guards	Roman soldiers
Three women	Mary of Magdala
	Mary, mother of James
	Salome
Shroud	Burial clothes

Also required are two (or three) sheets of paper with the following sentences to be completed:
– Mary (called Magdalene) from whom . . . . had come out.
– Near . . . . of Jesus stood his mother, his mother's sister, Mary the wife of Clopas, and Mary Magdalene.
– Mary Magdalene and the other Mary were sitting there opposite the . . . .
– Mary Magdalene went to the . . . . with the news: "I have seen the Lord."

The corresponding texts should also be given:
John 20:18   Luke 8:2
John 19:25   Matthew 27:61

An unused, redundant roll of wallpaper approximately 5–6ft long. Sufficient drawing and colouring materials.

PREPARATION:

As above.

OPENING ACTIVITY:

(The children are arranged in two or three teams, mixing the ages. Each team is given the six words in the left-hand column as well as the four texts. They must first find at least two of the pairs in the room, then sit together and complete the sentences, using their bibles for the four texts.)

NEW WORDS:

Resurrection – When Jesus rose from the dead on Easter Sunday morning.
Appearances– When Jesus was seen alive by his friends after his resurrection.

PRESENTATION:

Let us look back at the texts that you completed in the opening activity. What did you learn about Mary Magdalene? *(Accept all the relevant information.)* What do you think was the most important moment in her life? A moment which was also important for *all* Christians? Yes, when she met the risen Jesus.

Someone suggested that it was Mary's presence at the death of Jesus on the cross. Yes, that was a very important moment, but not so important as the resurrection appearance. If Jesus had died and not risen from the dead, we would not be sitting here today, because there would have been no Christian Church.

TEXT:	*Early on Sunday morning, while it was still dark,* *Mary Magdalene went to the tomb and saw that* *the stone had been taken away from the entrance.* John 20:1

Has anyone any idea why Mary was chosen to have the privilege of finding the tomb empty, and was the first to see Jesus alive again? *(Accept any ideas and develop them.)* The simple answer is that we do not know, but it might have been because, while the men friends of Jesus ran away and left him (apart from John) to die alone, the women friends were faithful and loyal. They were rewarded by God the Father by being the first witnesses of the resurrection of Jesus; and Mary was the most important of the group. So Mary's proudest moment must have been when she realized that she had been chosen by God to be the first to meet the risen Jesus.

PRACTICAL
ACTIVITY:

Let's return to the words used for the "pairs". In twos or threes, choose one word, for example "guards" or "tomb", and draw and colour it. *(Guidance will be necessary on relative sizes.)* We will stick these on the long paper to make a frieze, illustrating the events of the first Easter morning.

BIBLE SEARCH:

(Bible search formed part of the opening activity so it may be omitted here. However, if thought desirable, the following may be used.)

There was another important witness to the truth of the resurrection of Jesus. Let us find out what happened to this other person, this time a man. Look up:

John 11:16

John 14:5

John 20:24–28

Write out, in your own words, *(younger pupils may need help)* what happened to Thomas; and finish with his short prayer (verse 28).

LOOKING
FORWARD:

None.

PSALM FOR
THE WEEK:

Give thanks to the LORD, because he is good,
and his love is eternal.
The stone which the builders rejected as worthless
turned out to be the most important of all.
This was done by the LORD;
what a wonderful sight it is!
This is the day of the LORD's victory;
let us be happy, let us celebrate! Psalm 118:1, 22–24

MEMORY
VERSE:

This is the day of the Lord's victory;
let us be happy, let us celebrate!

CLOSING
HYMN:

> He is Lord   JP75/MP69
> Majesty   JP60/MP151
> This is the day   JP255/MP239
> Led like a lamb   JP151/MP282
> Alleluia, Alleluia, give thanks to the risen Lord   JP3/MP9

LESSON 28: *The Beloved Disciple*

<table>
<tr>
<td>AIM:</td>
<td>To help the children to understand the great importance of developing our love of God, so that they can all appreciate that we are each called to be a "beloved disciple".</td>
</tr>
<tr>
<td>AIDS:</td>
<td>Pieces of white cardboard or stiff paper, suitable for making cards with; enough for one each. Colouring pencils, crayons, etc. A roll of unused wallpaper, long enough to contain the responses needed for the "Presentation".</td>
</tr>
<tr>
<td>PREPARATION:</td>
<td>Using the roll of unused wallpaper (reverse side) write out in large, clear letters the responses needed or the "Presentation". Space them 9in. (20cm) apart. Only unroll it as each response is required, so that only at the end will every response be seen.</td>
</tr>
<tr>
<td>OPENING ACTIVITY:</td>
<td>

(Give out the cards and direct the children to fold them in half.) I want you all to draw a large heart on the front of your card and inside write the words "I love you".

When you have done that I want you to think about who you are going to give it to and for what occasion. For example, are you thinking of it as a Mother's Day card? or a birthday card? or Valentine card? or for some other occasion or person? When you have decided you can, if you wish, write the person's name on the front, or inside. *(Ask each pupil who their card is for, and make appreciative comments where possible.)*

We have heard several people mentioned: mothers, grandparents, boyfriends . . . but no one has made a card for Jesus. We say that we love Jesus, but when we really start thinking and talking about love, we never naturally include him. Why?
</td>
</tr>
<tr>
<td>NEW WORDS:</td>
<td>

We have learnt many new words in previous lessons. Today we will have a little test to see how well you remember some of the more important ones:

Providence   Messiah
Covenant   Stewardship
</td>
</tr>
<tr>
<td>PRESENTATION:</td>
<td>

Let us all use our bibles to look up Matthew 4:21–22. Jesus called John and his brother James to follow him; they left the boat and their father, Zebedee, and followed him. John was faced with a choice – should he stay with his father and his job as a fisherman, or leave it all behind and follow Jesus.

Response: Love is answering God's call. *(Unroll wallpaper "banner".)*

Now let's all look up in our bibles Luke 9:28–33. Jesus took John, with Peter and James, to a quiet place on a mountain to pray, and while they were there Jesus appeared to shine with a bright light and was seen talking with the prophet Elijah and Moses, the Lawgiver.

Response: Love is sharing your secrets with a friend. *(Unroll the next section of the "banner".)*

We will now find the text John 13:23. John sits so close to Jesus at the Last Supper, that by laying his head back it was resting on Jesus.

Response: Love is wanting to stay close to your friend. *(Unroll banner.)*

Our next text is John 19:25–27. With death very close, Jesus commits his mother into the care of John, his beloved friend.
</td>
</tr>
</table>

TEXT: *One of them, the one whom Jesus loved, was sitting next to Jesus . . .*
So that disciple moved closer to Jesus' side and asked, ''Who is it, Lord?''
John 13:23, 25

Response: Love is trusting your most precious possession to your friend. *(Unroll banner.)*

Finally let us look up John 20:1–9. Mary Magdalene finds the tomb empty and tells the disciples. Peter and John run to the tomb and find the burial clothes of Jesus. John sees and believes that Jesus has risen.

Response: Love is accepting God's truth when most people reject it. *(Unroll the last section of the banner.)*

John the evangelist is the apostle who writes most about God's love for us and our love of God. We will see this in our Bible search.

PRACTICAL
ACTIVITY:
On the sheet of plain paper provided choose one of the ''Love is . . .'' captions that we have just talked about. Copy it neatly in the centre and decorate all round the border.

BIBLE SEARCH:
We have used our bibles more than usual this session so we will concentrate on only one text: John 4:7–21.
Find out: How many times the words ''love'' ''loves'' or ''loved'' are mentioned *(Twenty-seven times).*
What love is (it is also the shortest sentence).
Who is a liar?

LOOKING
BACKWARDS:
Christians know that Jesus told us to love God and our neighbour. However, we should realize that hundreds of years before Jesus was born Moses told the Jewish people:
''Love the Lord your God with all your heart and with all your soul and with all your strength.''
Deuteronomy 6:5

PSALM FOR
THE WEEK:
I pray to you, O God, because you answer me;
so turn to me and listen to my words.
Reveal your wonderful love and save me;
at your side I am safe from our enemies.
Protect me as you would your very eyes;
hide me in the shadow of your wings. Psalm 17:6–8

MEMORY
VERSE:
Protect me as you would your very eyes;
hide me in the shadow of your wings.

CLOSING
HYMN:

He brought me to his banqueting house   JP73
Jesus' love is very wonderful   JP139
I'm very glad of God   JP107
The greatest thing in all my life   JP239

LESSON 29: *Simon Peter, the Big Fisherman*

AIM: To help the children to understand the importance of faith as the entrance qualification to the Christian community (the Church).

AIDS: If possible a copy, perhaps from a local library, of *The Big Fisherman* by Lloyd C. Douglas. One empty washing-up liquid bottle, or a similar plastic bottle; scissors and glue; a straw; a piece of white paper; and plasticine or Blu-tack.

PREPARATION: Prepare a list of possible nicknames for the pupils. It must be stressed when talking with them that the names are not serious, and just for fun. If a real, personal example can be given by the teacher, that will help. Prepare slips of paper with the twelve texts required for the Bible search.

OPENING ACTIVITY: Has anyone here got a nickname at home or school? For example, when I was at school I was called . . . . Sometimes a nickname starts because of how we look, or what we wear, or something that we do. For *fun* I have made up some nicknames for you all. Here they are:

NEW WORDS:

Faith – This word has two very closely connected meanings: First, it means to believe; my faith is what I believe in. Second, it means to trust; so if you believe in someone you trust them. In the life of the Christian the word carries both meanings: when I say I have faith in the Lord Jesus, it means I believe that Jesus is the Lord, and that I trust him fully.

Church – This word can mean the community of all Christian believers world-wide; or it can mean the local community of believers in a particular neighbourhood; or it can mean the building in which the Christian community meets. It also can refer to a particular part of the Christian family: so we can speak of the Methodist Church or the United Reformed Church.

BIBLE SEARCH: We are going to have our Bible search earlier in the lesson today. We are going to look for people whose names were changed. For each text you must find out the name of the person in the beginning and then what it was changed to:
Genesis 32:27–28
Acts 13:9
Names were sometimes changed in the Bible when God had an important part for the person to play.

(Each child is given a slip of paper with one of the following texts on it. The slips are numbered because that is the order in which they will be read out.)

We are now going to learn a little of the life of Simon Peter. Look up the text you are given. When asked to do so, either tell us what it says about Simon Peter or read out the text.

1. Matthew 4:18–22
2. Matthew 10:1–4
3. Matthew 16:13–20
4. Luke 8:49–56
7. Mark 14:27–31
8. Luke 22:31–37
9. Matthew 26:69–75
10. John 20:1–9

Simon Peter answered, "You are the Messiah, the Son of the living God."
"Good for you, Simon son of John!" answered Jesus . . . "I tell you, Peter:
you are a rock, and on this rock foundation I will build my church."

Matthew 16:16–18

5. Matthew 17:1–13   11. John 21:15–23
6. Matthew 17:24–27   12. Acts 3:1–10

(If there are more than twelve children, more texts can be found in Acts, or the younger pupils may double-up with older ones.)

PRESENTATION: I would like to start with a little reading from a very famous book, *The Big Fisherman*. Chapter 5 has an imaginative description of Simon Peter.

Alone on the broad tiller-seat of The Abigail (a three-masted fishing boat) a gigantic, hairy, deeply tanned Galilean of thirty-five – as busy with his awl as were his employees – occasionally looked up to survey their work . . . It was obvious that the relation of the master and his men was cordial . . . for it was a testimonial to a man's seamanship if he was signed on to sail under Simon, the son of Jonah.

Among the Galileans the name of Simon was so common that it had to be tagged for better identification. Every Simon bore a special designation: Simon the tanner, Simon the weaver, Simon the little . . . But, to the neighbours and relatives who had known him since childhood, he was Simon, the son of Jonah. It was inevitable, however, that the huge, noisy, quick-tempered, lamentably irreverent son of Jonah should become known by a more colourful name . . . In the country round about, Simon, the Son of Jonah, was referred to as the Big Fisherman.

That reading is not from the Bible; it is based upon information from the Bible and other sources from the time of Jesus.

There is much in the life of Simon Peter that we could concentrate on: his denial of Jesus and forgiveness, or his preaching after the resurrection of Jesus. We are thinking today of his faith.

(Read again the opening text.) Lloyd C. Douglas in his book, *The Big Fisherman*, describes that moment in Simon's life like this *(chapter 15)*:

Making no reference to the dangerous miracle Jesus had performed (curing a group of lepers), he continued to speak about the security of a life that is lived by faith. There was, he said, two habitations from which to choose one's place of spiritual residence. One of these houses was built upon the rock of faith: the rain might pour in torrents and the tempest might rage; but that house would stand firm, for it was founded upon a rock . . . "Upon a *petros*," he added (using the Greek word). The other house was built upon the sand: it might be good for fair weather, but it could not survive a storm.

Later that evening the apostles were talking about who the crowd thought Jesus was. "Almost everyone seems to think," said John, "that Jesus must be one of the ancient prophets restored to life."

At this point in the conversation, held in subdued tones to avoid disturbing the Master's much-needed rest, they were suddenly startled by his voice, inquiring, "And you? What do you think of me? Who am I?"

They all shifted their eyes to Simon, whose courageous display of faith that afternoon (when the lepers had been cured) had earned him the right to be their

75

spokesman. After a long, thoughtful pause, the Big Fisherman came to his feet and declared, in a deep, impressive voice, "Master – I believe that you are the Son of God." A hush fell upon them.

"Simon, son of Jonah," said Jesus, "henceforth your name shall be Peter – Peter the Rock. It is upon your faith that I shall build my Kingdom."

So Jesus gave Simon the nickname "the Rock", or in the language that the gospels were written in, *petros*. So you can see how he came to be called Simon Peter and, later in his life, just Peter.

The lesson for us all from Simon Peter's life is that our faith is very, very important. The whole of our lives, as Christians, is built upon it.

PRACTICAL
ACTIVITY:

Let us make Peter's fishing boat. Cut the bottle in half along its length (*Adult help will be required with this.*) Take one half and press in a small ball of plasticine or Blue-tack into the middle of the bottom of the boat. Fold the white paper in half to form a triangular sail. Leaving about 2in of the straw sticking out, glue the straw-mast in the fold of the sail. Push the "sail" upright into the plasticine. It's time to launch Peter's fishing boat!

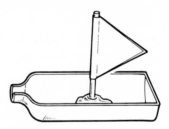

(*For homework the pupils can be asked to finish the boat off by equipping it with a net and a figure of Peter. A successful prize for the best boat, brought to the next class, could be a stick of rock or some other hard, sticky candy.*)

LOOKING
FORWARD:

None.

PSALM FOR
THE WEEK:

I will always thank the LORD;
I will never stop praising him.
I will praise him for what he has done;
may all who are oppressed listen and be glad!
Proclaim with me the LORD's greatness;
let us praise his name together!
                                    Psalm 34:1–3

MEMORY
VERSE:

Proclaim with me the Lord's greatness;
let us praise his name together.

CLOSING
HYMN:

Big man standing by the blue waterside   JP16
I will make you fishers of men   JP23
Peter and James and John in a sailboat   JP197
God forgave my sin in Jesus' name   JP54

LESSON 30:   *The Night-Time Friend*

AIM: To help the children appreciate the meaning of Jesus' words, "unless you are born again of water . . .", and the importance of Baptism for the Christian community.

AIDS: Dark glasses for all the class, or one pupil brought into the room blindfold. A few packets of cress seeds and several saucers or low dishes (preferably enough for one each); tissue paper or sheets of toilet paper, or pieces of flannel material. Paper, scissors, colouring pens or pencils.

PREPARATION: The idea is for all the class to experience what it is like to be without clear sight. Either all put on dark glasses (indoors it will be hard to see with them); or one volunteer comes in as a blind person, then talks about what it was like to be sightless for a while.

OPENING ACTIVITY: *(As outlined above.)* We have now gained a little insight into what it is like to be unable to see clearly. Let us look at our text for today again:

". . . a member of the Jewish ruling Council" – they were hostile and opposed to Jesus. They were blind to the true meaning of what Jesus was preaching.

"One night" – John tells us that Nicodemus came to see Jesus in the dark, when it is not easy to see.

In his reply to Nicodemus Jesus says, "No one can *see* the kingdom of God unless he is born again."

The message is clear: the person who accepts the teaching of Jesus, who wants to enter the kingdom of God, can see: he or she is no longer stumbling around in the dark.

Let us now listen to a reading:

Somewhere behind the dark clouds, something stirred. One hundred and eighty brightly dressed children stared hopefully at the distant, dark horizon. This was Tromso, Norway – 215 miles inside the Arctic Circle and, for the past two months, in permanent darkness. Now, at eight minutes to midday, the sun was due back. Not for long, mind you – four minutes only on the first day.

The bells pealed out and hundreds of colourful balloons were sent flying high into the gloom. They had been looking forward to this moment since last 25 November when the wan winter sun had finally sunk from view. This was Sun Day, for the children a day off school; a celebration declared by King Olav in 1873. *(Daily Mail)*

Can you imagine that? Living in total darkness, except for artificial light, for two whole months? The people of the most northerly city in the world have to do that every year.

NEW WORD: Baptism – The outward and visible sign of conversion, and the joining of the Christian family. At first it took place by the person being immersed in water, and some Christian communities continue with that method. Some Christian communities pour the water on a child's head. Both actions are accompanied by an invocation to the Holy Trinity.

PRESENTATION: Blind, how hard it would be to be blind. How hard it must be, too, to live in the town of Tromso where two whole months go past with no daylight.

The Jewish leaders did not like Jesus. They did not believe that he came from God and

78

would not accept his message. Worse than that, they actually plotted to kill Jesus. If goodness is light, then the Jewish leaders were definitely living in the dark. Nicodemus was one of the Jewish Council – he came from the dark side. Jesus spoke to him and told him how he could accept the light . . . which he did.

Then Jesus spoke of Baptism: how a person, who accepts Jesus as the Light of the World, can belong to the community of those who have accepted the Good News that Jesus preached. Let's listen again to what Jesus said to Nicodemus: John 3:1–21.

Not easy to understand, is it? But did you notice the words of Jesus about light and darkness? Jesus also says, "No one can enter the kingdom of God unless he is born of water and the Spirit." It is by the waters of Baptism that we enter the new life of the Spirit.

PRACTICAL ACTIVITY:

(There are two activities: the first is more suited to the younger members and the second to the older, but they are interchangeable.)

(To illustrate the importance of water for life and growth.) Set up the dishes with the absorbent material lying in bottom and quite a thick sprinkling of seeds on top. Then water them thoroughly. *(Pupils are entrusted with one each to take home, with strict instructions to put the dish in a bright place and water every morning and evening. They must bring them back next time to show the others.)*

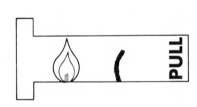

Let's first find John 8:12 in the Bible. Now we're going to make candles.

(As the accompanying diagram shows, the plan is to make a candle, with a pull slip which "lights" it. Using an A4 sheet of paper/card – the paper used needs to be quite stiff, or use light card – cut a 2in. strip off one end. Take ¼in. off each side of the slip but leave ½ in. either side, as a "stop" bar. Leave a space at the top and bottom of the large sheet, for words. Cut three slits, about 1½in. apart, as shown. Now draw the candle to finish, with the wick just into the space between the first and second slit, from left. At the top of the sheet write: Jesus said, "I am; and under the candle write: the light of the world." On the pull slip, write "pull" on the far right, and draw and colour a flame on the first 1½in. of the slip. Assemble. Adult help will be required throughout.)

BIBLE SEARCH:

We have included Nicodemus as a friend of Jesus, but we have not seen how he was a friend. Look up the following and write out the words that show that Nicodemus was a friend to Jesus:

John 7:45–52   John 19:38–42

LOOKING FORWARD:

None.

PSALM FOR THE WEEK:

O Lord, you give me light;
  you dispel my darkness.
You give me strength to attack my enemies
  and power to overcome their defences.

This God – how perfect are his deeds!
  How dependable his words!
He is like a shield
  for all who seek his protection. Psalm 18:28–30

MEMORY VERSE:

O Lord, you give me light; you dispel my darkness.

CLOSING HYMN:

God forgave my sin in Jesus' name   JP54
Colours of Day   JP28
Father we adore you   JP44
For I'm building a people of power   JP47
This little light of mine   JP258

LESSON 31: # The Little Man in the Tree

AIM:

To help the children appreciate that if we, like Zacchaeus, repent of any wrong doing, we will deepen our friendship with Jesus, not lose it.

AIDS:

(The story of Zacchaeus easily lends itself to dramatization by the children.)
A pair of step ladders, the taller the better. Speaker/teacher's tax returns or pay slip, which gives details of tax deducted at source. A safe but visible place where s/he can burn pieces of paper: a dustbin or metal waste bin. Paper and pencils.

PREPARATION:

The children playing the parts of Jesus and Zacchaeus need to be carefully chosen. "Jesus" should be tall and with a "presence"; "Zacchaeus" has to be one of the smallest of the children.

OPENING ACTIVITY:

(First read the story to the children: Luke 19:1–10. Ask them to act it out, helping them to cast the play and suggesting where the action will start, as Jesus will be moving and talking to people. The "tree" is the step-ladder, which can be used in its original condition or decorated for the part it plays. Zacchaeus runs ahead and climbs it; peers over the top and is seen by Jesus and invited down.)

NEW WORDS:

Repentance – Being sorry for some wrong that has been done.
Reconciliation – To make up with someone after there has been a conflict or separation.

PRESENTATION:

(Exhibit, without necessarily revealing the detail, the tax return or pay slip.) This piece of paper tells me how much I must pay the Government in taxes; your parents have something similar, too. Why do adults complain about paying taxes? What is it about taxes that upsets grown-ups? *(Accept all answers.)* So the Government is not very popular when it makes us pay money from our earnings, especially if it raises taxes.

Can you imagine how we would all feel if the taxes we paid were not used for our benefit but were paid to a foreign army and sent out of the country? That is what happened in the time of Jesus because the money went to the despised Romans.

The Romans had a clever way of collecting the taxes. They used greedy Jews who wanted to get rich quick. These Jewish tax collectors made a lot of money for themselves by charging the people extra. Now perhaps you can understand why tax collectors were so hated by good Jews and thought to be the worst of sinners. Zacchaeus was one of those tax collectors. That is why the crowd were so upset:

All the people saw this [Jesus going to Zacchaeus' house for dinner] and began to mutter, "He has gone to be the guest of a 'sinner'." (Luke 19:7).

Zacchaeus repents. He offers to give back the money that he has cheated people of and he is sorry; he is reconciled with God. Through the acceptance of Jesus, Zacchaeus is reconciled with God. He wants to be reconciled with the people, but that may take quite a while, until they are convinced that he really has given up his greedy ways.

PRACTICAL ACTIVITY:

(Give out pieces of paper and pencils.) I want the older ones among you now to help the younger ones (there will be no help from adults). On the piece of paper write down anything that you are sorry for; that has damaged your friendship with God, and/or your family. For example, if you were cheeky and rude to your mum or dad.

So Zacchaeus ran ahead of the crowd and climbed a sycamore tree to see Jesus, who was going to pass that way. Luke 19:4

If you are really sorry for what you have written, and all the other wrong things that you have done, come forward and put your folded paper here. *(Indicate the dustbin lid or receptacle where the paper is to be burnt. When the paper is gathered say a simple prayer, like the following:)*

Loving Father, you are much quicker to forgive us than we are to forgive one another. Like Zacchaeus we say "sorry" for all the wrong we have done. May the burning of our papers mark the beginning of a new effort to love and serve you. May we forgive one another as you so promptly forgive us. Amen.

(Light the papers and dampen the fire completely when all have burned.)

BIBLE SEARCH: Look up the following and write out what you find:

Matthew 6:12   Luke 6:37
Luke 6:27   John 8:11
Matthew 18:21–22

LOOKING BACKWARD: In the times before Jesus, Old Testament times, the Jewish people had one way of showing that their sins had been taken away: they used the scapegoat. Let us look at that together: Leviticus 16:20–22.

PSALM FOR THE WEEK:

Be merciful to me, O God,
  because of your constant love.
Because of your great mercy
  wipe away my sins!
Wash away all my evil
  and make me clean from my sin! Psalm 51:1–2

MEMORY VERSE:

Be merciful to me, O God,
  because of your constant love.

CLOSING HYMN:

Zacchaeus was a very little man   JP300
Cleanse me from my sin, Lord   JP27
One more step along the world I go   JP188
God forgave my sin in Jesus' name   JP54

The Converted Pharisee

AIM:	To inspire the children by the example of Paul to think of themselves as missionaries for the Good News, as he was.
AIDS:	All modern translations have maps of Paul's missionary journeys – Good News, NIV, etc. Each pupil needs sight of one. Also of value is *New World* by Alan Dale (OUP). His summary of Paul's work, pp.219–23, is excellent. Poster-size paper and colouring pens.
PREPARATION:	Put the children into groups of three or four, mixing the ages.
OPENING ACTIVITY:	In your groups talk for a little while about bullying at school. For example, has anyone in your group been bullied? Then make up a little play, to show the rest of us – just a short one – about a bully who changed into being a good, helpful person. *(Allow about five minutes for this, then watch each presentation.)* Let us now listen to the story of Saul, who was a Pharisee (a strict Jew) and a bully. He changed into a great apostle and friend of Jesus: Acts 9:1–19. *(This reading could, with little difficulty, be adapted into a part reading; or a dramatized version could be used.)*
NEW WORDS:	Convert — Someone who changes his or her beliefs and way of life. Evangelize Evangelization } – To preach the Gospel of Jesus. Evangelist — One of the four gospel writers. An Evangelist — A Christian preacher who proclaims the Gospel.
PRESENTATION:	We know more about Paul's life and work than any of the other friends of Jesus. There is so much, that we can only consider a little of it now. Paul was a great missionary – he was also a great letter-writer and thinker. Let us now find the map which shows us where Paul travelled to spread the Good News of Jesus. Except for the voyages he took sometimes – and the shipwrecks – you must realize that he WALKED most of the distances involved, from town to town and city to city. While we listen to the following reading try to find the places mentioned on the map: Alan Dale's *New World* (pp.219–23, "The Crowded Years") or 2 Corinthians 11:21, 23–8. Paul was a very brave and very hard-working evangelist, but he could only use his voice to spread the teaching of Jesus. He did write letters but they were to Christian communities that he had founded. What methods could he use today?
PRACTICAL ACTIVITY:	Return to the groups you had at the beginning of the lesson and make a list of the methods Paul could use if he were preaching today. You have seen posters advertising modern evangelists. Design one advertising Paul as a visiting preacher to your town, or as appearing soon on television or a radio programme.
BIBLE SEARCH:	How much can you learn about Paul from the following? (Remember that his name was Saul at first.)

TEXT: *And pray also for me, that whenever I open my mouth, words may be given*
         me so that I will fearlessly make known the mystery of the gospel,
         for which I am an ambassador in chains.   Ephesians 6:19

Acts 7:57–66   Acts 16:22–40
Acts 22:2–5   Acts 28:1–6
Acts 28:11–16

LOOKING   None.
FORWARD:

PSALM FOR   *I will proclaim your greatness, my God and king;*
THE WEEK: *I will thank you for ever and ever.*
            Every day I will thank you;
                I will praise you for ever and ever.
            The LORD is great and is to be highly praised;
                his greatness is beyond understanding.

            What you have done will be praised
                from one generation to the next;
                they will proclaim your mighty acts. Psalm 145:1–4

MEMORY   *Every day I will thank you;*
VERSE: *I will praise you for ever and ever.*

CLOSING   ┌──┐
HYMN: │   Colours of day dawn into the mind   JP28   │
            │   All over the world the Spirit is moving   JP5   │
            │   How lovely on the mountains are the feet of him   JP84│
            │   Remember all the people   JP207   │
            └──┘

The Unwilling Helper

AIM: To help the children to understand and appreciate that by helping at unexpected times and in unexpected circumstances we are helping and serving Christ.

AIDS: Stiff, white card or thin board, A4 size, to make masks. Also lengths of elastic.

PREPARATION: A good reader.

OPENING ACTIVITY:

We know little about Simon from Cyrene except that he was forced to carry the cross of Jesus; and his sons, Alexander and Rufus, were known to the Christian community in Rome (where Mark wrote his gospel).

Simon did a kindness for a stranger. There is a famous story from our Christian heritage which we should all know. It is about Martin of Tours, who as a medic (as we call them these days) serving with the Roman Army, wanted to become a Christian. His life was written 1,590 years ago by a Christian writer called Sulpicius Severus. The reading is taken from that life, written in the year 400 A D.

At a certain period, when Martin had nothing except his arms and simple military dress in the middle of the winter, a winter which had shown itself more severe than ordinary so that the extreme cold was proving fatal to many, Martin happened to meet, at the gate of the city of Amiens, a poor man destitute of clothing. He was entreating those that passed by to have compassion on him, but all passed the wretched man without notice. Martin recognized that it was left to him to help. Yet what should he do? He had nothing except for his large army cloak. Taking his sword he divided his cloak into two equal parts, and gave one part to the poor man, while he again clothed himself with the remainder. Upon this some of the bystanders laughed at him because he was now such an unsightly object, and stood out as but partly dressed.

The following night, when Martin had resigned himself to sleep, he had a vision of Christ who was dressed in that part of his cloak which he had given to the poor man. He heard Jesus saying with a clear voice to the multitude of angels standing around: "Martin clothed me with his cloak."

Martin left the Roman Army, was baptized and eventually became Bishop of Tours and a missionary. After his death he was venerated as a saint. Very famous throughout Europe, many churches were named after him, like St Martin-in-the-Fields in central London.

NEW WORDS: Voluntary – Some work to help others is called "voluntary" work. It means work that is done freely, without pay or anything in exchange.

Charity – This word is the English version of *caritas* which is Latin for "love". In older bibles you can find the word "charity" where now the word "love" is used; for example, look up 1 Corinthians 13 in the Authorised Version (King James). In more recent times the word is used for a Charity, that is an organization that uses voluntary work to raise money for the needy.

PRACTICAL ACTIVITY: *(Moved here as part of the preparation for the Presentation. The masks to be made are going to be two-sided: on one side the face of a sheep/goat and on the reverse a smiley face/unhappy face. Half of*

TEXT:	*On the way they met a man named Simon, who was coming into the city from the country, and the soldiers forced him to carry Jesus' cross. (Simon was from Cyrene and was the father of Alexander and Rufus.)* Mark 15:21

	the children should draw the face of a sheep, with a smiley face on the reverse; half draw a goat, with an unhappy face on the other side.)
PRESENTATION:	One of the parables that Jesus told links very closely with the story of Simon of Cyrene and Martin of Tours. It is the parable of the sheep and the goats. Let us now read and act it out: Matthew 25:31–46. *(This can be presented as a play, using the masks for the herd, and then for the "righteous", smiley face, and "unrighteous"; or as a mime – the adult leader/teacher can be the "King"; or as a dramatized reading.)*
	As our presentation is finished, take off your masks. Who was the King representing in the story? When will all this take place? Hands up all those who hope that they will be "sheep" on that day? How can we, with God's help, be "sheep"?
	"Whatever you did for one of the least of these brothers of mine, you did for me" *(Matthew 25–40)*. When Simon was pulled by the Roman soldiers from the crowd to carry the cross of Jesus, he probably did not know Jesus. He would not have known that he was carrying the cross for the Son of God. His family were known to the Christians of Rome, so Simon probably became a follower of Jesus. Martin also did a kindness for a stranger and became a Christian.
BIBLE SEARCH:	The thought that what we do for others, we do for Christ himself can be found in other places in the Bible. Look up and write out the following:
	Matthew 10:40
	Hebrews 13:2
	Acts 9:1–5
	Notice how, in the vision that Saul has, Christ does not say, "Why do you persecute my followers?" He actually says, "Why do you persecute ME?"
LOOKING FORWARD:	None.
PSALM FOR THE WEEK:	*The LORD is loving and merciful, slow to become angry and full of constant love. He is good to everyone and has compassion on all he made.*
	All your creatures, LORD, will praise you, and all your people will give you thanks. Psalm 145:8–10
MEMORY VERSE:	*All your creatures, Lord, will praise you.*
CLOSING HYMN:	When I needed a neighbour JP275 Make me a channel of your peace JP161 Love, joy, peace and patience, kindness JP158

The Friend who Doubted

AIM:
To help the children to appreciate that, while it is natural to doubt, with God's help we can believe the truths of the Christian faith.

AIDS:
A poster with, written large, the words – SEEING IS BELIEVING. Two volunteers to hold up the poster when required. They stand in full view. Required for each pupil: scissors; plain white paper, 7in. × 7in.; a piece of soft wood for a stick, approx 14in. long (must be *soft* wood: bamboo, for example, will not work); a nail with a flat head; colouring pencils or pens.
(It is important that the teacher makes a poster at home first.)

PREPARATION:
The Bible text, John 20:19–31, can be easily read in parts. Either use a dramatized version or divide up the text, with the following parts: narrator, Jesus, Thomas, the disciples (three voices together). For a smooth reading it is wise to practise with the group first.

OPENING ACTIVITY:
I am going to read out a number of objects: some are real things or places, some are not real. If you have seen the item, either with your own eyes or in a picture, call out "seen it" and our two helpers will hold up the poster. If I call out an object or place no one has seen, or it cannot be seen, then the poster is put down.

Here we go:

Tower Bridge	Edinburgh Castle
a kangaroo	Never-Never Land
Concord	a dodo
the white cliffs of Dover	
a dinosaur's bones	the wind
(Add more if desired.)	

Three of those no one could see; which were they? Never-Never Land is a make-believe land in the story of *Peter Pan*; the dodo is an extinct bird; and the wind cannot be seen, only felt. But we will talk more about that later.

NEW WORDS:
Conviction – Holding a belief very firmly to be true.

Evidence   – Facts that show something to be true or false.

PRESENTATION:
(The dramatized John 20:19–31, as prepared.) "Unless I see the nail marks in his hands", Thomas said. He would not believe because he could not see. Thomas would have said, "Seeing is believing; if I can't see something I will not believe in it."

I want you to turn to your friend sitting next to you and talk for one minute about this. Did Thomas really trust his eyes? What would Thomas have said if he had been a blind man? *(Allow no more than a minute, then ask each pair in turn.)* The correct answer is that Thomas was so doubtful that he did not even trust his eyes, he wanted to touch as well:

"Unless I put my finger where the nails were, and put my hand into his side . . ."

Seeing is believing. In our Opening activity we had a problem about the wind: the wind cannot be seen. We can see what the wind *does* when it blows paper up the street or makes the branches of the trees rustle and sway, but we cannot SEE the wind itself. It is the same with electricity, which we all use every day. We know what it does, we know how it is made with great generators, but it is impossible to see. Although you can make it

TEXT:	*Jesus said to Thomas, "Put your finger here and look at my hands; then stretch out your hand and put it in my side. Stop your doubting, and believe!"* John 20:27

spark, or light a bulb, etc. it cannot be seen. The wind is real; electricity is real. Seeing is not believing.

Love is real. We know what it is, but it is not easy to describe. We know how people behave when they are in love; there are signs too that we can all recognize. But no one has ever seen love; just as no one has ever seen God.

So when people say to us, "seeing is believing", remember the wind, remember electricity and remember love. They are all real but cannot be seen. Then remember Thomas and his words, "My Lord and my God."

Now we are going to write out, so that we do not forget, the reply Jesus gave to Thomas:

"Do you believe because you see me? How happy are those who believe without seeing me!"

Jesus is speaking of you and me, for we have not seen the risen Jesus, but we believe.

PRACTICAL ACTIVITY: Let's make something that we can use in the wind, to remind us that the wind, like God, is invisible but powerful. We're going to make windmills, following a simple diagram. Colour each "sail" of the windmill before hammering the nail through the sails, gathered together in the middle. (*Adult supervision and help is required at the final stage.*)

BIBLE SEARCH: Look up the following: John 11:16 and John 14:5–7. Now decide which eighteen words of Jesus' that you have just found best illustrates the words of Thomas: "My Lord and my God."

LOOKING FORWARD: None.

PSALM FOR THE WEEK:
Proclaim with me the LORD's greatness;
* let us praise his name together!*

I prayed to the LORD, and he answered me;
* he freed me from all my fears.*
The oppressed look to him and are glad;
* they will never be disappointed.* Psalm 34:3–5

MEMORY VERSE:
Proclaim with me the Lord's greatness.

CLOSING HYMN:

> Seek ye first the kingdom of God   JP215
> Ask, ask, ask and it shall be given you   JP11
> Amazing Grace   JP8/MP10
> God forgave my sin in Jesus' name   JP54

LESSON 35: *The First-Called Disciple*

AIM:
To help the children to understand that, like Andrew, we are all called to be disciples and to answer the Lord every day when he says, "Come".

AIDS:
A length of netting (if fishing net is not available then the black type used by gardeners to cover soft fruit or, failing that, a length of net curtain). White paper and, if possible, fish templates for the younger ones; scissors and colouring pens.

PREPARATION:
Make sufficient simple invitations for each of the pupils; they should, if possible be properly typed and laid out. Wording could be something like:

(Name of pupil)
You
are invited to
a meeting with Jesus
on (date of the lesson)
at (place where lesson is held)

OPENING ACTIVITY:
(When the pupils have arrived the invitations are given out, without comment. As soon as all have had an opportunity to read the invitation . . .) I cannot say, "I hope you will *come*," because you have *come*: you are here. Listen to the two Bible texts now to be read.

"Where two or three *come* together in my name, I am there with them." *(Matthew 18:20)*

That means that Jesus is here with us now.

"*Come*, follow me," Jesus said, "and I will make you fishers of men." *(Matthew 4:19)*

"Come" is an invitation. Jesus invites his followers to be fishers of men. Who can tell me who those words were first spoken to? Yes, Andrew and his brother Simon.

NEW WORD:
Disciple – A disciple is a person who faithfully follows a religious teacher to learn a way of life.

PRESENTATION:
Andrew was a fisherman. Who can tell me the answers to the following questions?
1. What was his brother's name?
2. What was his father's name?
3. Where did Andrew fish?
4. Andrew was the disciple of another teacher before Jesus; who?

Jesus told Andrew and Simon that he would make them "fishers of men". Was Jesus himself a fisher of men? Yes, of course; he drew people to him and they faithfully followed him.

PRACTICAL ACTIVITY:
We will pretend that this length of netting is Andrew's fishing net, which he used from his father Zebedee's boat on the sea of Galilee. We will drape it on this wall and you can be "fish" caught in the net.
Draw the shape of a fish on the sheet of white paper; write your name, as big as you can; and colour round the edges. When you have cut it out, go and attach it to the net by hooking the fins, tail or head into the net.

TEXT:	*Andrew, Simon Peter's brother, was one of the two who heard what John had said and who had followed Jesus.* John 1:40

Has anyone been fishing? There are two types of fishing: fresh water fishing and sea fishing. Both use rather different methods to catch the fish. Both methods have something on the end of the line to attract the fish. The fish swimming in the sea, or in a river, are attracted by food, either a worm or a fly. If we are to be "fishers of men", like the apostle Andrew, what can we use to attract people with? Any ideas? *(Accept suggestions.)*

When the apostles were telling people about Jesus, and many were "caught" in the net, the pagans used to say, "See how these Christians love one another." They were attracted to the Christian faith because it seemed to make people better people. The love the Christians had for others was attractive. Do people notice how loving you are? Does our love for one another attract people to follow Jesus? Our bait is ourselves. If we are kind, thoughtful, caring and obviously devoted to following Jesus, then people will be attracted to what they see is good and brings lasting happiness.

BIBLE SEARCH: How much can we find out about the apostle Andrew?

Matthew 4:18	Mark 1:16
Mark 1:29	John 6:8
John 12:20–22	

LOOKING FORWARD: Next lesson we will have a little test on the different people we have read about and learned about over the past twelve lessons.

PSALM FOR THE WEEK:

Give thanks to the LORD, proclaim his greatness;
    tell the nations what he has done.
Sing praise to the LORD;
    tell of the wonderful things he has done.
Be glad that we belong to him;
    let all who worship him rejoice. Psalm 105:1–3

MEMORY VERSE: *Let all who worship him rejoice.*

CLOSING HYMN:

I will make you fishers of men   JP123
Peter, James and John in a sailboat   JP197
Big man standing by the blue waterside   JP16
I have decided to follow Jesus   JP98

The Disciple who Despaired

AIM:	To help the children to understand that no matter what dreadful sin(s) they might, in the future, commit, if they are truly sorry God will forgive them.
AIDS:	Thirty cardboard discs, measuring 2in. (5cm) in diameter, need to be cut out and ready; thirty pieces of silver tinfoil of 2½in. (6cm) in diameter. A pen or pencil for each pupil. A flat surface for the children to work on. Two older children to volunteer to play the roles of Simon Peter and Judas.
PREPARATION:	As above.
OPENING ACTIVITY:	*(The cardboard discs and small sheets of foil are given out. If there are less than thirty children, give the eldest more than one; if there are more than thirty, give the discs to the older pupils. It does not matter if pupils have several "coins".)*

You know the story of Judas, how he betrayed Jesus for thirty silver coins. Let us hear what the gospel writer, Matthew said: Matthew 26:14–16.

With the card and silver foil let us now make "silver" coins. Before you make your "coin"(s) take the pencil(pen) and write in the centre of the cardboard some wrongdoing that you have done. We commit a "sin" when we fail to live up to the ideals set for us by Jesus; when we break one of the Commandments. Now write down one sin that you are sorry for. Perhaps you have told a lie, or taken something that has not belonged to you, or ignored what your mother asked you to do or been disrespectful to her. Perhaps you have been cruel to a brother or sister, or let a friend down, or spread gossip about someone.

When you have written down one sin, place the card in the middle of the foil, with your writing facing you, and fold over the edges. Smooth out the "silver" side.

Judas failed in a very big way; he committed a very big sin. We do not usually commit very big sins, but we still fail God every day by committing small sins. (We will need our "coins" later.)

NEW WORDS:	Perseverance – To keep steadily holding on to your beliefs; keeping close to God no matter what happens.
	Despair – To give up all hope.
PRESENTATION:	There were two disciples who failed: one betrayed Jesus to the Jewish leaders, the other denied even knowing Jesus. The first was Judas and *(name)* is taking his part. The second was Simon Peter and *(name)* is reading his part. Let us compare the two disciples who failed Jesus. *("Peter" reads his first statement, followed by "Judas" and so on. Both should stand out in the front for all to see.)*

Peter:	I was chosen as a friend of Jesus.	*Judas:*	I was chosen as a friend of Jesus.
Peter:	I was trusted by Jesus.	*Judas:*	I was trusted by Jesus.
Peter:	I walked all over Galilee with Jesus.	*Judas:*	I walked all over Galilee with Jesus.
Peter:	We slept out, rough, in the country together.	*Judas:*	We slept out, rough, in the country together.

TEXT:

*Then one of the twelve disciples – the one named Judas Iscariot –
went to the chief priests and asked, "What will you give me
if I betray Jesus to you?"*   Matthew 26:14–15

Peter: I swore that I did not even know Jesus.

Judas: I betrayed Jesus for money.

Peter: I was very ashamed of what I had done.

Judas: I was very ashamed of what I had done.

Peter: I hoped for forgiveness.

Judas: I despaired of being forgiven.

Peter: I told Jesus that I loved him and was sorry.

Judas: In my despair I killed myself.

Peter believed that Jesus would forgive him, and Jesus did forgive him and made him the leader of his apostles. Judas did not believe that he could be forgiven, he despaired and took his life. Peter had perseverance and his faith was rewarded, but Judas had nothing but despair. If we ever do a very bad thing we must persevere in our belief that Jesus will forgive us, as he forgave Peter and would have forgiven Judas, if he had asked for forgiveness.

(*"Peter" now collects all the thirty "coins" and "Judas" sits down.*) Peter will choose six of the "coins" a selection of different sins) and read them out. After each, we will say the words of Peter when he said sorry for what he had done, "Lord, you know that we love you."

PRACTICAL
ACTIVITY:
None.

BIBLE SEARCH:
To learn a little more about Judas Iscariot (there were other followers called Judas), look up the following:

John 12:4–5   John 13:7
John 13:21–30   John 18:2–11
Matthew 27:3–5

EVALUATION:
Last week I promised that we would have a little test on the people we have met in the last twelve lessons:
1. What was the name of Simon and Andrew's father?
2. Who did Andrew follow before he became a disciple of Jesus?
3. What nickname was Simon given?
4. Who was the brother of Martha and Mary?
5. Who was "the Beloved disciple"?
6. What was the name of the tax collector who climbed the tree?
7. Complete the missing name: "man from Cyrene . . . . . ., the father of Alexander and Rufus."
8. To whom did Jesus say, "Stop doubting and believe"?
9. Who was Zebedee?
10. Which apostles wrote gospels?

PSALM FOR
THE WEEK:

Praise the Lord, my soul;
    all my being, praise his holy name.
Praise the Lord, my soul,
    and do not forget how kind he is.
He forgives all my sins
    and heals all my diseases,
He keeps me from the grave
    and blesses me with love and mercy.
He fills my life with good things,
    so that I stay young and strong like an eagle. Psalm 103:1–5

MEMORY
VERSE:

Praise the Lord, my soul;
    all my being, praise his holy name.

CLOSING
HYMN:

Big man standing by the blue waterside   JP16
God forgave my sin   JP54
Ask, Ask, Ask, and it shall be given you   JP11
I sing a song of the saints of God   JP115

Scripture Index

15:1–7
15:8–10
15:11–24
19:1–10
19:4
19:28–40
22:14–30
8:2
8:49–56
12:24
22:3–6
22:31–37

John
1:1
1:5
3:5
3:10
3:1–2
6:8
7:45–52
8:11
8:12
10:11
10:14
11:1
11:16

12:1–8
12:12–16
12:19
12:20–22
13:1
13:21–30
13:23
14:5–7
14:27
15:20
18:2–11
19:25
19:25–27
19:38–42
20:19–31
20:27
20:1
20:1–9
20:18
20:24–28
21:15–23

Acts
2:1–12
3:1–10
7:57–66
7:59–60

9:2
9:1–9
10:1–2
13:9
16:22–40
16:33
22:2–5
28:1–6
28:11–16

Romans
8:19–21
5:12–21
12:14

1 Corinthians
11:7
12

Galatians
5:22
6:9–10

Ephesians
2:20–22
5:15–16
6:19

Colossians
1:4
4:5

Hebrews
10:22
13:2

1 Peter
5:4

2 Peter
2:1
2:15–16

1 John
3:12
4:7–21

Revelation
12:9
12:14
20:2
22:5